FOR ORGANS, PIANOS & ELECTRONIC KEYBOARDS

E•Z PLAY TODAY

398

Selections From

Disney's

PRINCESS

Collections

W9-CRP-614

Belle 3
Can You Feel the Love Tonight 15
Colors of the Wind 18
A Dream Is a Wish Your Heart Makes 24
Forget About Love 30
Home 40
I Won't Say (I'm in Love) 26
I Wonder 46
If I Can't Love Her 51
Just Around the Riverbend 59
Kiss the Girl 67
Love 48
Once Upon a Dream 64
Out of Thin Air 72
Part of Your World 79
Reflection 87
Sleeping Beauty 90
So This Is Love (The Cinderella Waltz) 92
Something There 94
A Whole New World 100

ISBN 0-634-01682-2

Walt Disney Music Company
Wonderland Music Company, Inc.

DISTRIBUTED BY

HAL•LEONARD®
CORPORATION

7777 W. BLUEMOUND RD. P.O. BOX 13819 MILWAUKEE, WI 53213

Visit Hal Leonard Online at
www.halleonard.com

BELLE
(Beauty and the Beast)
Lyrics by Howard Ashman
Music by Alan Menken

Little town, it's a quiet village.
Every day like the one before.
Little town full of little people
Waking up to say:

Bonjour! Bonjour!
Bonjour! Bonjour! Bonjour!

There goes the baker with his tray, like always,
The same old bread and rolls to sell.
Every morning just the same
Since the morning that we came
To this poor provincial town.

Look, there she goes, that girl is strange, no question.
Dazed and distracted, can't you tell?
Never part of any crowd,
'Cause her head's up on some cloud.
No denying she's a funny girl, that Belle.

Bonjour.
Good day.
How is your family?
Bonjour.
Good day.
How is your wife?
I need six eggs!
That's too expensive.
There must be more than this provincial life.

Look, there she goes, that girl is so peculiar.
I wonder if she's feeling well.
With a dreamy, far–off look
And her nose stuck in a book,
What a puzzle to the rest of us is Belle.

Oh, isn't this amazing?
It's my favorite part because…you'll see.
Here's where she meets Prince Charming,
But she won't discover that it's him 'til chapter three.

Now, it's no wonder that her name means "beauty."
Her looks have got no parallel.
But behind that fair facade,
I'm afraid she's rather odd.
Very different from the rest of us.
She's nothing like the rest of us.
Yes, different from the rest of us is Belle.

Right from the moment when I met her, saw her,
I said she's gorgeous and I fell.
Here in town there's only she
Who is beautiful as me,
So I'm making plans to woo and marry Belle.

Look, there he goes!
Isn't he dreamy?
Monsieur Gaston!
Oh, he's so cute!
Be still, my heart!
I'm hardly breathing!
He's such a tall, dark, strong and handsome brute.

Bonjour.
Pardon.
Good day.
Mais oui!
You call this bacon?
What lovely grapes!
Some cheese…
Ten yards.
One pound…
'Scuse me!
I'll get the knife.
Please let me through!
This bread…
Those fish…
It's stale!
They smell!
Madame's mistaken.

There must be more than this provincial life!
Just watch, I'm going to make Belle my wife!

Look, there she goes, a girl who's strange but special,
A most peculiar mademoiselle.
It's a pity and a sin.
She doesn't quite fit in
'Cause she really is a funny girl.
A beauty but a funny girl.
She really is a funny girl, that Belle!

Belle
from Walt Disney's BEAUTY AND THE BEAST

Registration 9
Rhythm: March or Polka

Lyrics by Howard Ashman
Music by Alan Menken

4

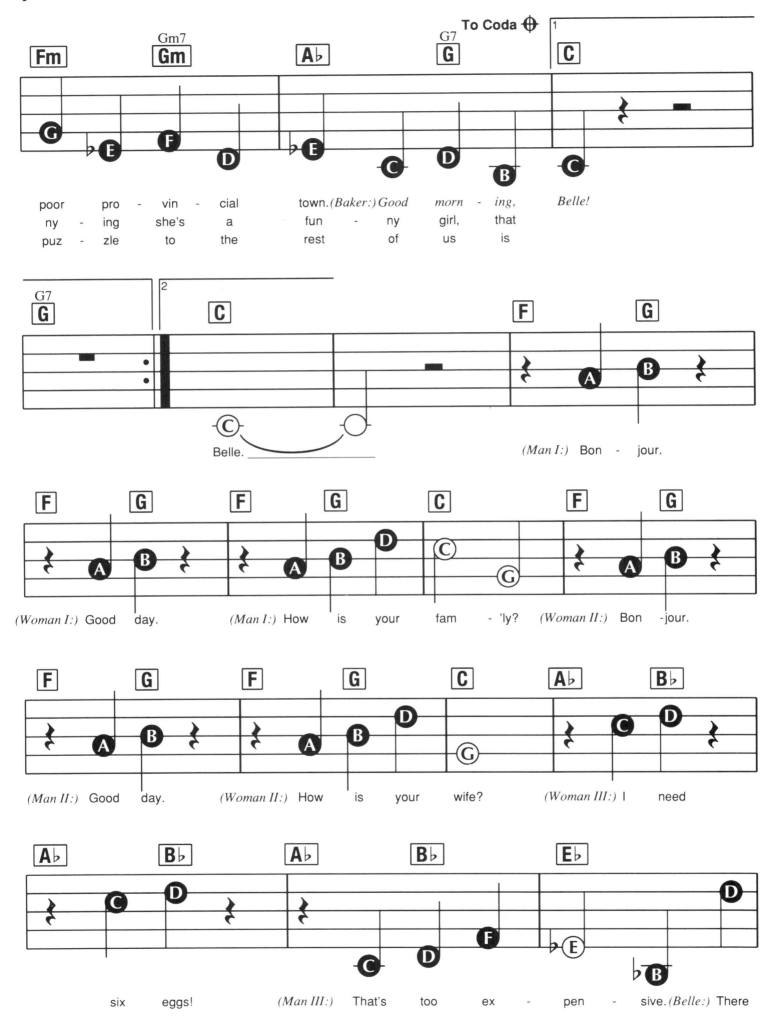

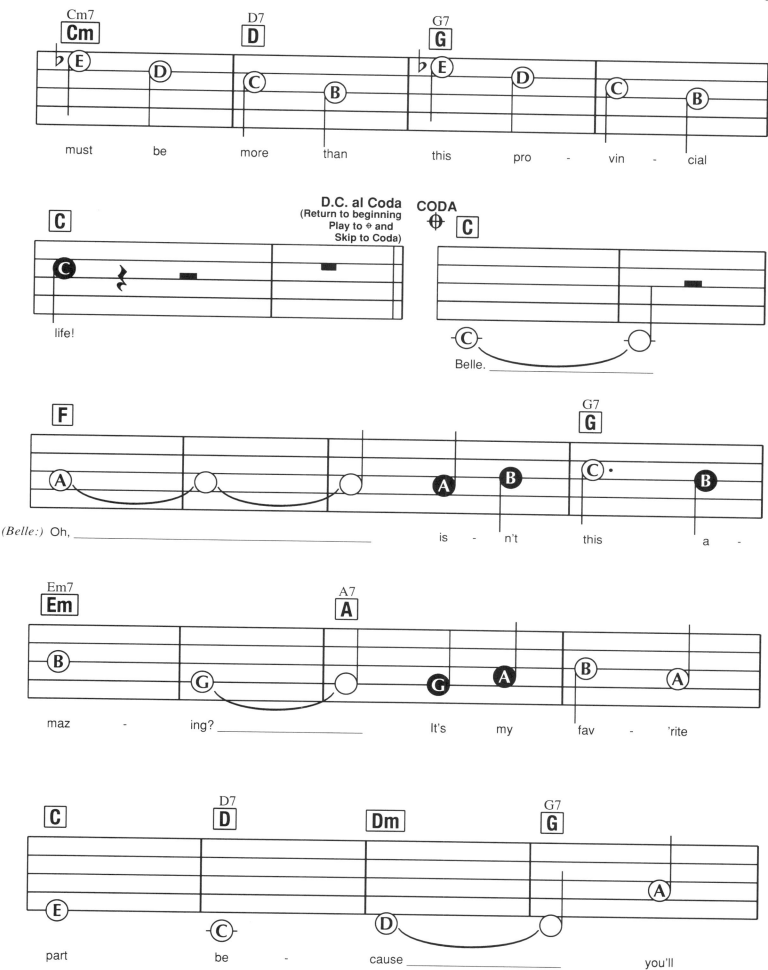

must be more than this pro - vin - cial

life!

D.C. al Coda
(Return to beginning
Play to ⊕ and
Skip to Coda)

CODA

Belle.

(Belle:) Oh, is - n't this a -

maz - ing? It's my fav - 'rite

part be - cause you'll

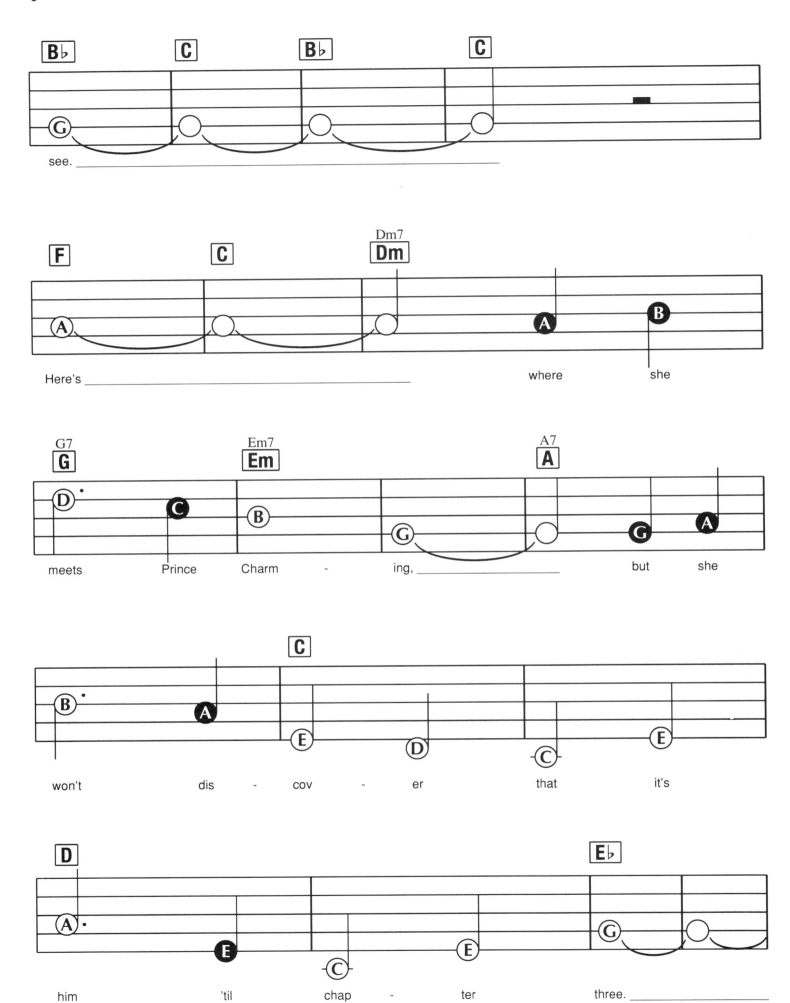

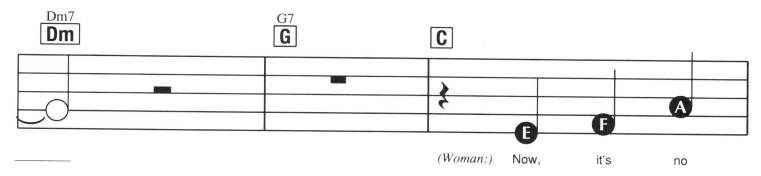

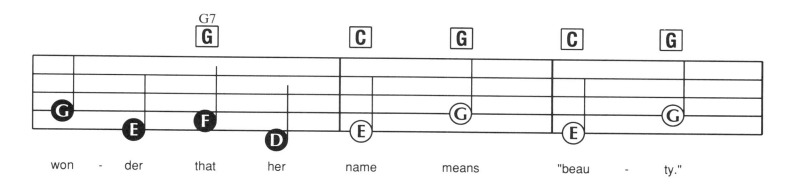

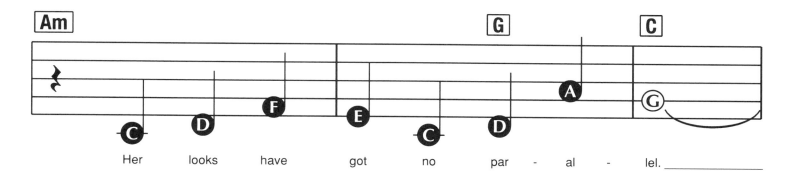

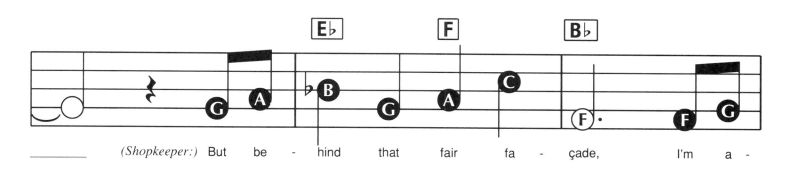

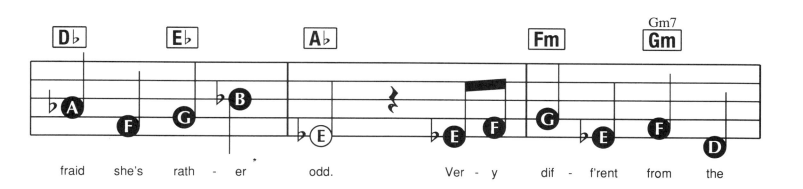

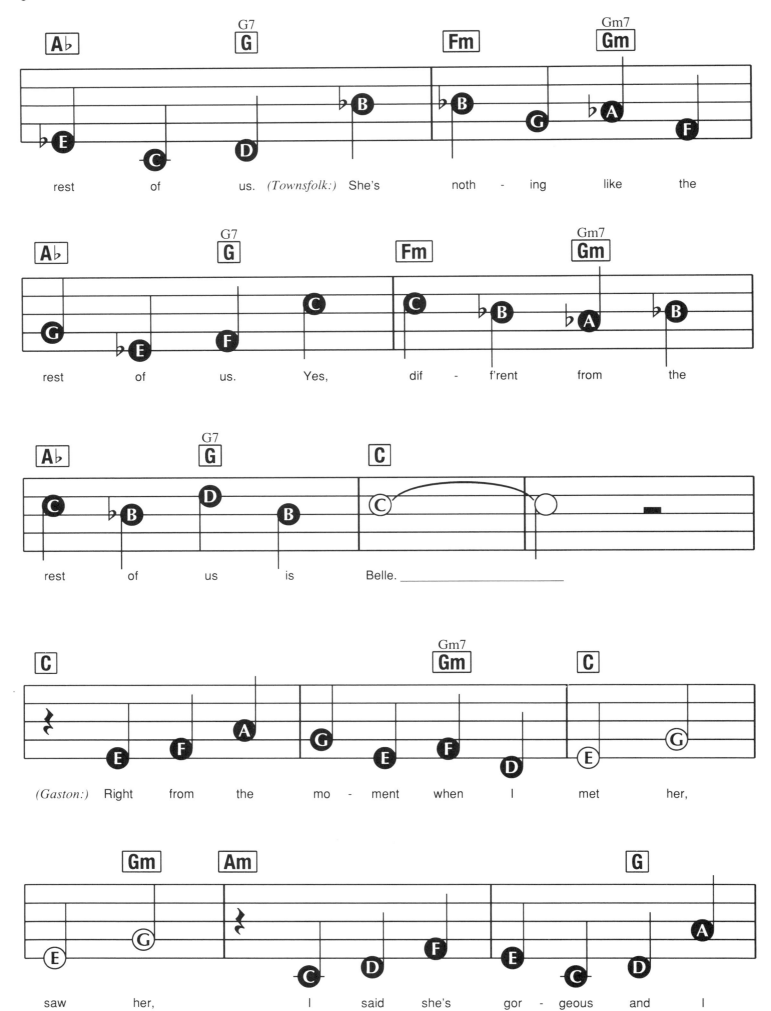

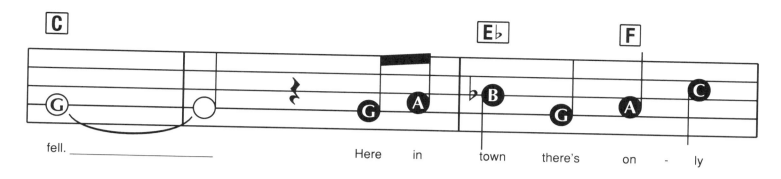

fell. _____ Here in town there's on - ly

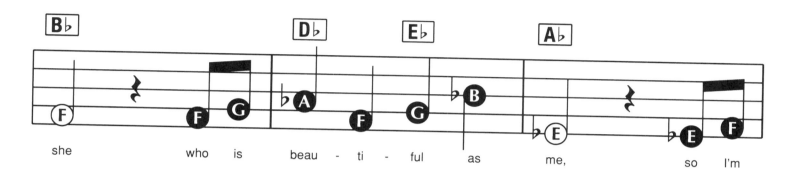

she who is beau - ti - ful as me, so I'm

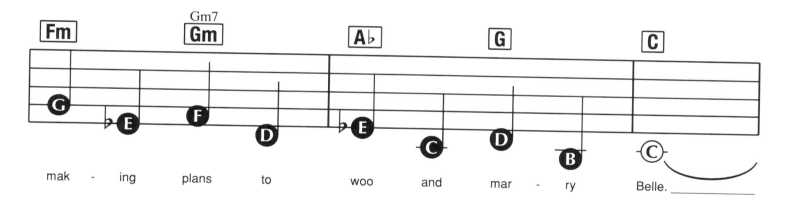

mak - ing plans to woo and mar - ry Belle. _____

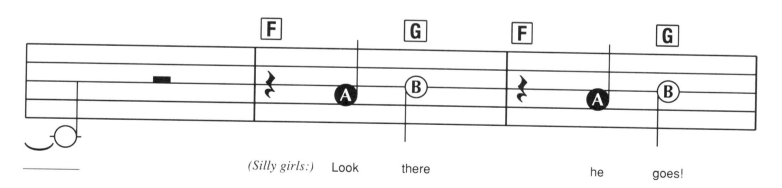

(Silly girls:) Look there he goes!

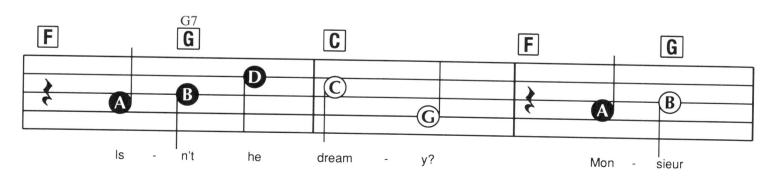

Is - n't he dream - y? Mon - sieur

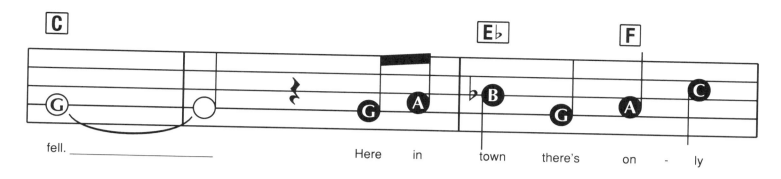

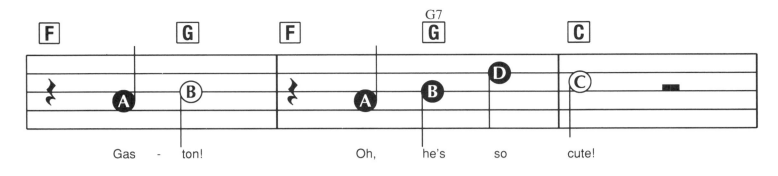

Gas - ton! Oh, he's so cute!

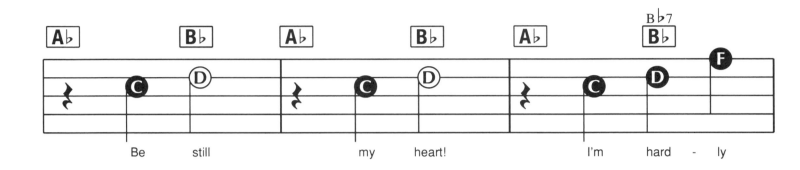

Be still my heart! I'm hard - ly

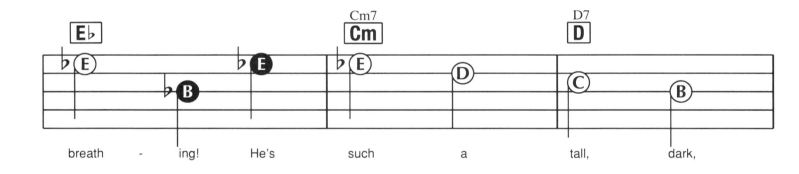

breath - ing! He's such a tall, dark,

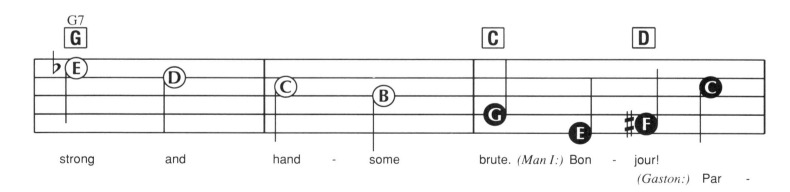

strong and hand - some brute. *(Man I:)* Bon - jour!

(Gaston:) Par -

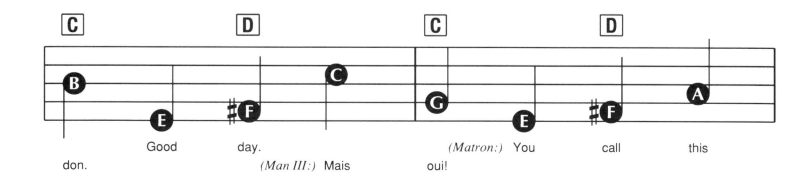

Good day.   *(Matron:)* You call this

don.   *(Man III:)* Mais oui!

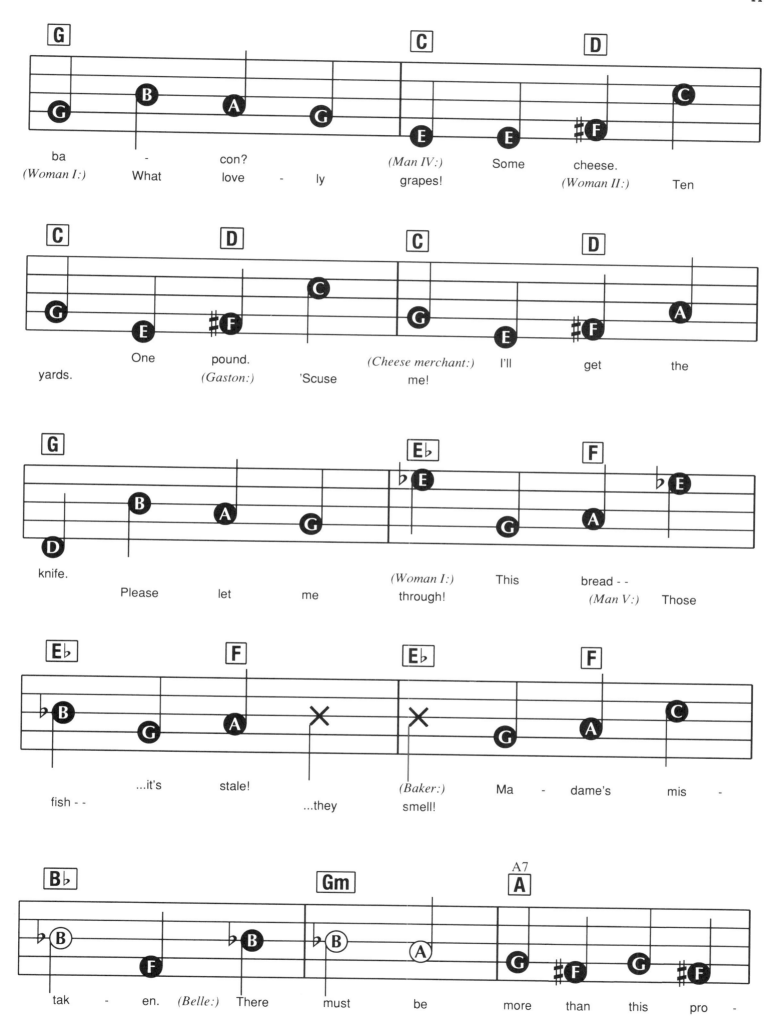

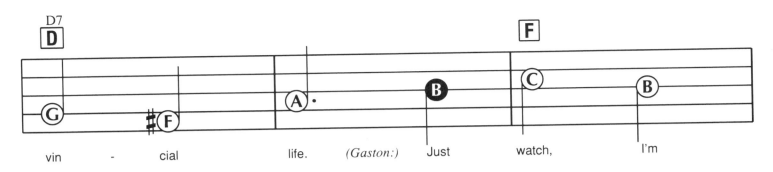

vin - cial life. *(Gaston:)* Just watch, I'm

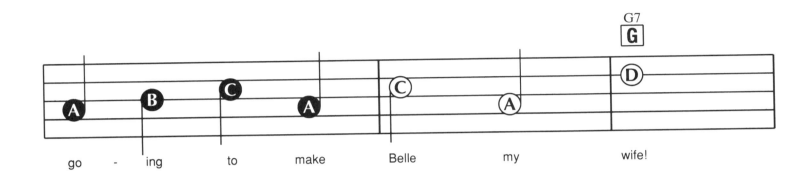

go - ing to make Belle my wife!

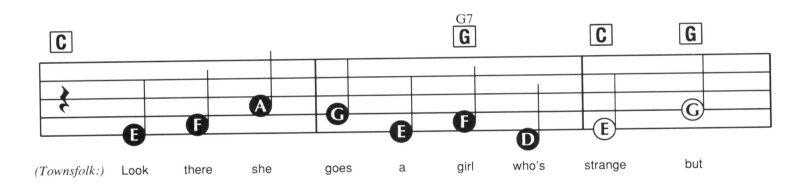

(Townsfolk:) Look there she goes a girl who's strange but

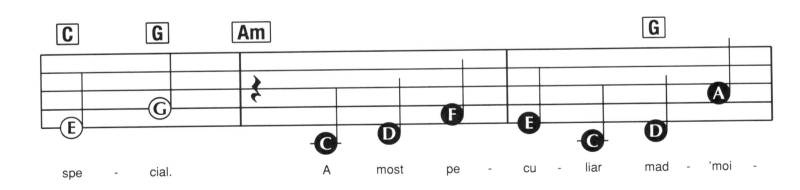

spe - cial. A most pe - cu - liar mad - 'moi -

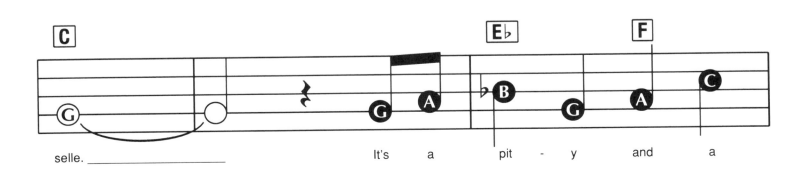

selle. _____ It's a pit - y and a

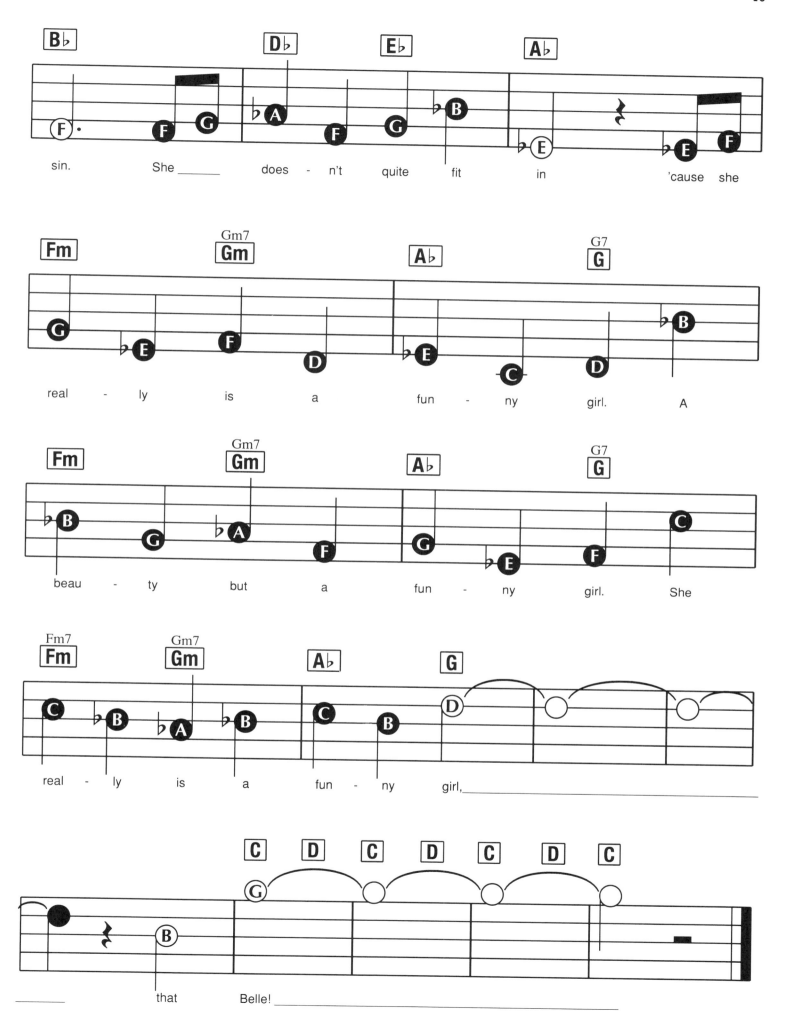

CAN YOU FEEL THE LOVE TONIGHT

(The Lion King)
Music by Elton John
Lyrics by Tim Rice

Timon
I can see what's happening
(Pumbaa: What?)
And they don't have a clue.
(Pumbaa: Who?)
They'll fall in love and here's the bottom line:
Our trio's down to two.
(Pumbaa: Oh.)

The sweet caress of twilight;
There's magic everywhere.
And with all this romantic atmosphere,
Disaster's in the air.

Chorus
Can you feel the love tonight,
The peace the evening brings?
The world, for once, in perfect harmony
With all its living things.

Simba
So many things to tell her,
But how to make her see
The truth about my past? Impossible.
She'd turn away from me.

Nala
He's holding back, he's hiding.
But what I can't decide.
Why won't he be the king I know he is,
The king I see inside?

Chorus
Can you feel the love tonight,
The peace the evening brings?
The world, for once, in perfect harmony
With all its living things.

Can you feel the love tonight?
You needn't look too far.
Stealing through the night's uncertainties,
Love is where they are.

Timon
And if he falls in love tonight,
It can be assumed

Pumbaa
His carefree days with us are history,

Timon & Pumbaa
In short, our pal is doomed.

COLORS OF THE WIND

(Pocahontas)
Music by Alan Menken
Lyrics by Stephen Schwartz

You think I'm an ignorant savage,
And you've been so many places,
I guess it must be so.
But still I cannot see,
If the savage one is me,
How can there be so much that you don't know?
You don't know...

You think you own whatever land you land on;
The earth is just a dead thing you can claim;
But I know ev'ry rock and tree and creature
Has a life, has a spirit, has a name.

You think the only people who are people
Are the people who look and think like you,
But if you walk the footsteps of a stranger
You'll learn things you never knew you never knew.

Have you ever heard the wolf cry to the blue corn moon,
Or asked the grinning bobcat why he grinned?
Can you sing with all the voices of the mountain?
Can you paint with all the colors of the wind?
Can you paint with all the colors of the wind?

Come run the hidden pine trails of the forest,
Come taste the sun-sweet berries of the earth;
Come roll in all the riches all around you,
And for once, never wonder what they're worth.

The rainstorm and the river are my brothers;
The heron and the otter are my friends;
And we are all connected to each other
In a circle, in a hoop that never ends.

How high does the sycamore grow?
If you cut it down, then you'll never know.

And you'll never hear the wolf cry to the blue corn moon,
For whether we are white or copper-skinned,
We need to sing with all the voices of the mountain,
Need to paint with all the colors of the wind.
You can own the earth and still
All you'll own is earth until
You can paint with all the colors of the wind.

Can You Feel the Love Tonight
from Walt Disney Pictures' THE LION KING

Registration 2
Rhythm: Rock or 8 Beat

Music by Elton John
Lyrics by Tim Rice

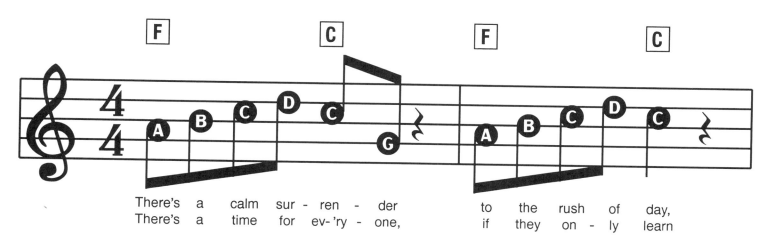

There's a calm sur-ren-der   to the rush of day,
There's a time for ev-'ry-one,   if they on-ly learn

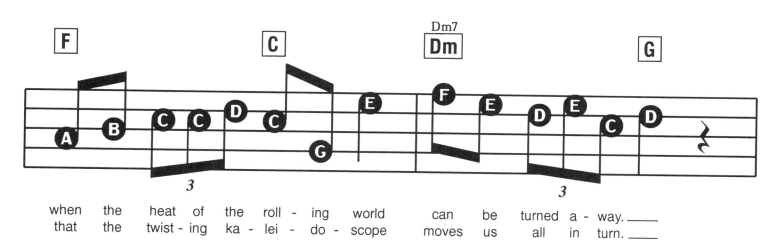

when the heat of the roll-ing world   can be turned a-way.____
that the twist-ing ka-lei-do-scope   moves us all in turn.____

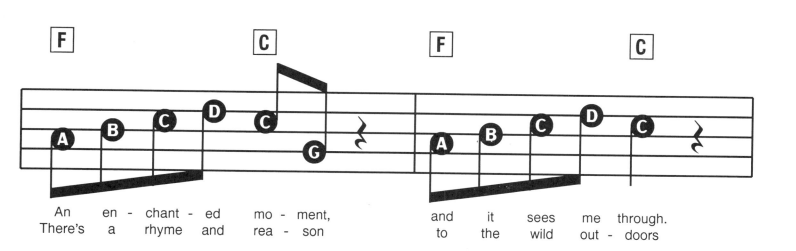

An en-chant-ed mo-ment,   and it sees me through.
There's a rhyme and rea-son   to the wild out-doors

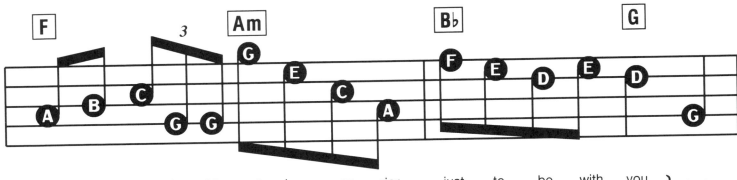

It's e - nough for this rest - less war - rior just to be with you. } And
when the heart of this star - crossed voy - ag - er beats in time with yours.

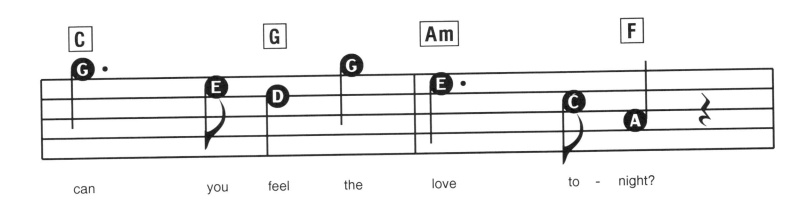

can you feel the love to - night?

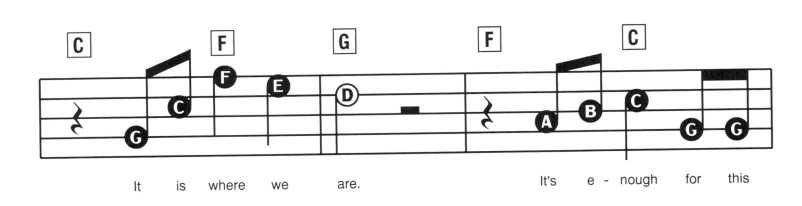

It is where we are. It's e - nough for this

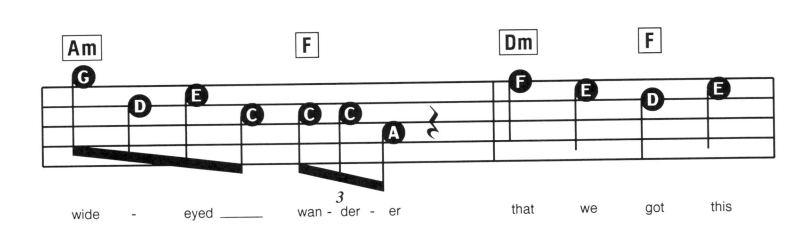

wide - eyed _____ wan - der - er that we got this

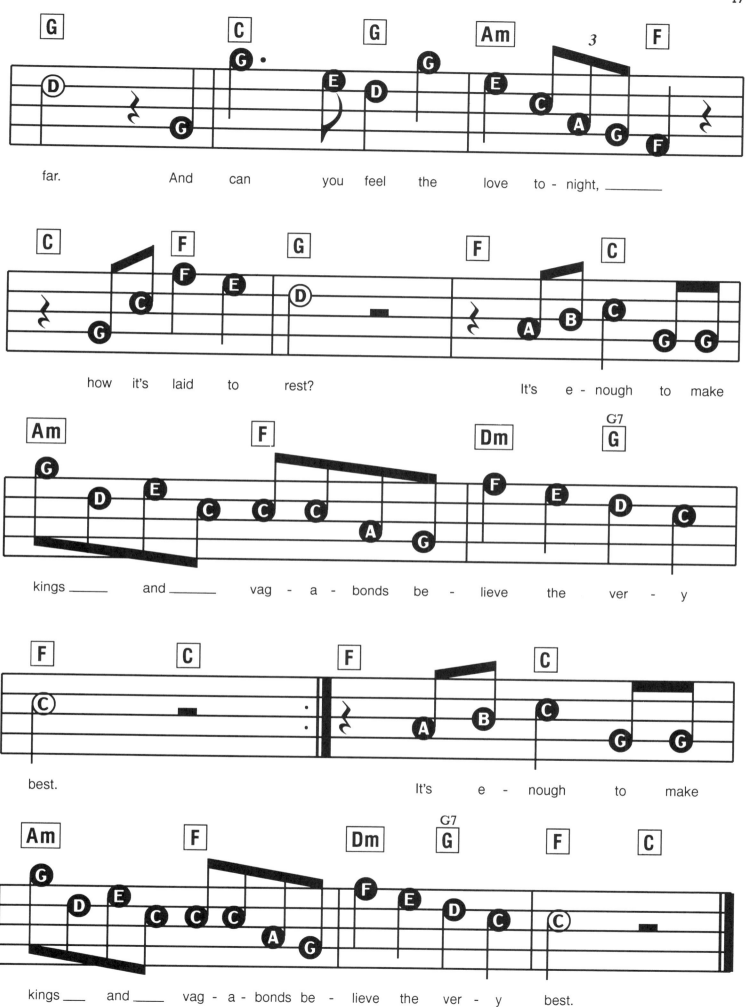

Colors of the Wind
from Walt Disney's POCAHONTAS

Registration 5
Rhythm: None

Music by Alan Menken
Lyrics by Stephen Schwartz

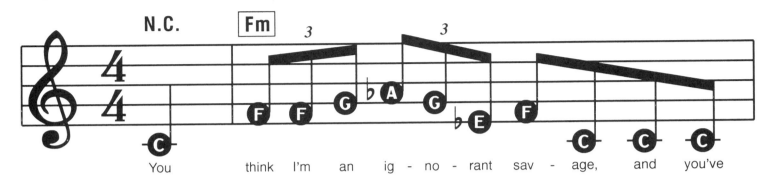

You think I'm an ig-no-rant sav-age, and you've

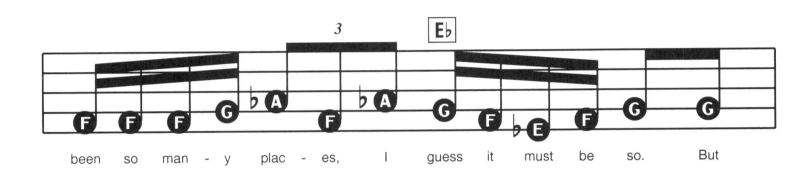

been so man-y plac-es, I guess it must be so. But

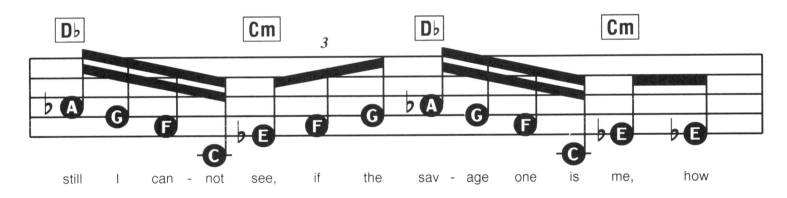

still I can-not see, if the sav-age one is me, how

Rhythm: Rock or 8-Beat

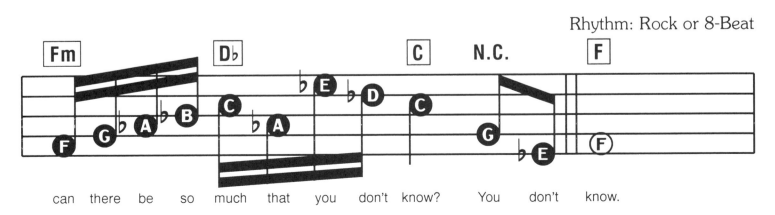

can there be so much that you don't know? You don't know.

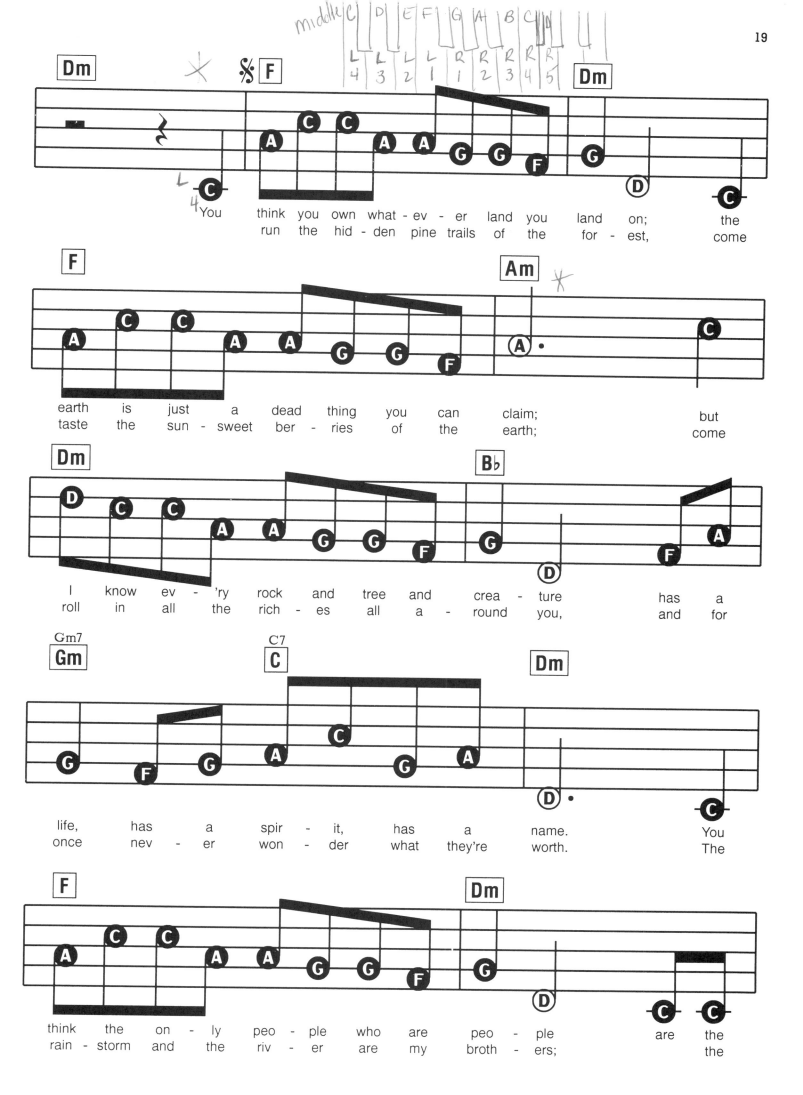

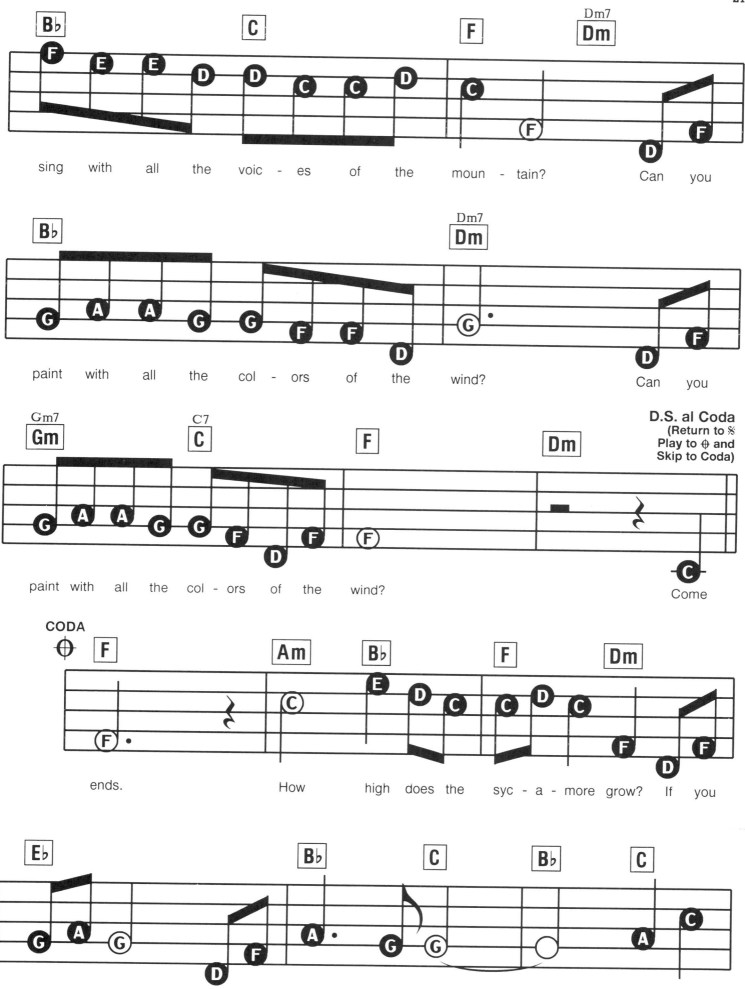

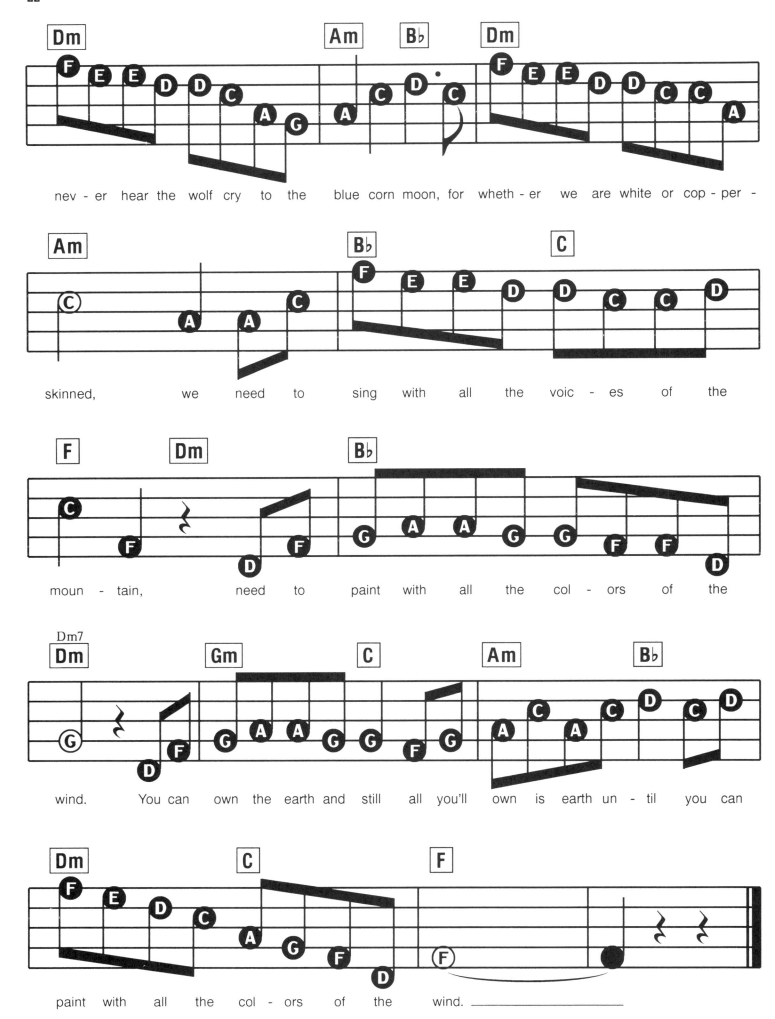

A DREAM IS A WISH YOUR HEART MAKES

(Cinderella)
Words and Music by Mack David,
Al Hoffman and Jerry Livingston

A dream is a wish your heart makes
When you're fast asleep.
In dreams you will lose your heartaches;
Whatever you wish for, you keep.
Have faith in your dreams and someday
Your rainbow will come smiling thru,
No matter how your heart is grieving,
If you keep on believing
The dream that you wish will come true.

...the dreams that I wish will come true.

No matter how your heart is grieving,
If you keep on believing
The dream that you wish will come true.

I WON'T SAY (I'M IN LOVE)

(Hercules)
Music by Alan Menken
Lyrics by David Zippel

Meg
If there's a prize for rotten judgment,
I guess I've already won that.
No man is worth the aggravation.
That's ancient history, been there, done that.

Muses
Who d'ya think you're kiddin',
He's the Earth and heaven to you.
Try to keep it hidden,
Honey, we can see right through you.
Girl, ya can't conceal it,
We know how ya feel and who you're thinking of.

Meg
No chance, no way, I won't say it, no, no.

Muses
You swoon, you sigh, why deny it, uh oh.

Meg
It's too cliché, I won't say I'm in love.

I thought my heart had learned its lesson.
It feels so good when you start out.
My head is screaming, get a grip, girl,
Unless you're dying to cry your heart out.

Muses
You keep on denying
Who you are and how you're feeling.
Baby, we're not buying,
Hon, we saw ya hit the ceiling.
Face it like a grown–up,
When ya gonna own up that ya got, got, got it bad.

Meg
No chance, no way, I won't say it, no, no.

Muses
Give up, give in. Check the grin, you're in love.

Meg
This scene won't play, I won't say I'm in love.

Muses
You're doin' flips, read our lips: You're in love.

Meg
You're way off base, I won't say it.
Get off my case, I won't say it.

Muses
Girl, don't be proud, it's O.K. you're in love.

Meg
Oh.
At least out loud, I won't say I'm in love.

A Dream Is a Wish Your Heart Makes
from Walt Disney's CINDERELLA

Registration 1
Rhythm: Fox Trot

Words and Music by Mack David,
Al Hoffman and Jerry Livingston

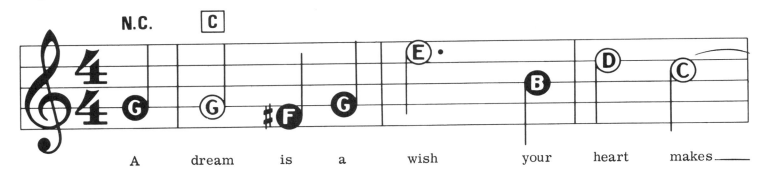

A dream is a wish your heart makes _____

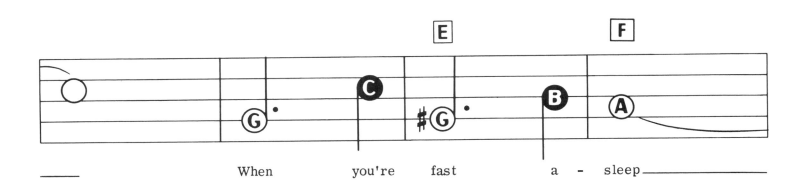

_____ When you're fast a - sleep _____

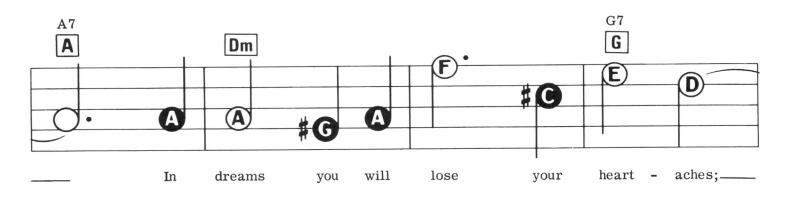

_____ In dreams you will lose your heart - aches; _____

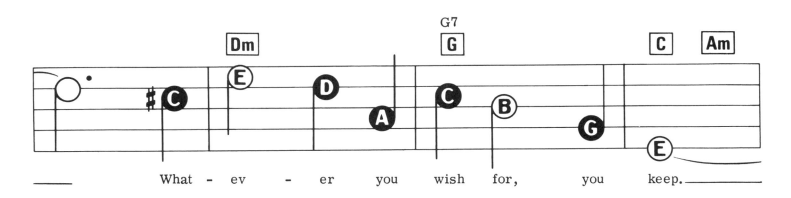

_____ What - ev - er you wish for, you keep. _____

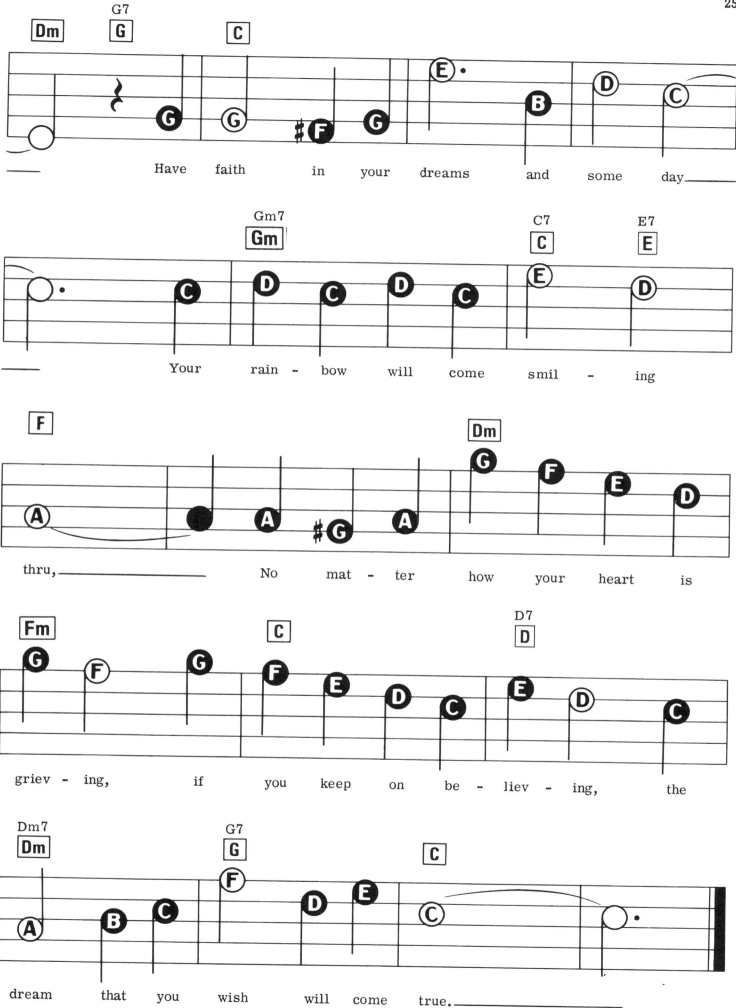

I Won't Say
(I'm in Love)
from Walt Disney Pictures' HERCULES

Registration 1
Rhythm: Pop or 8 Beat

Music by Alan Menken
Lyrics by David Zippel

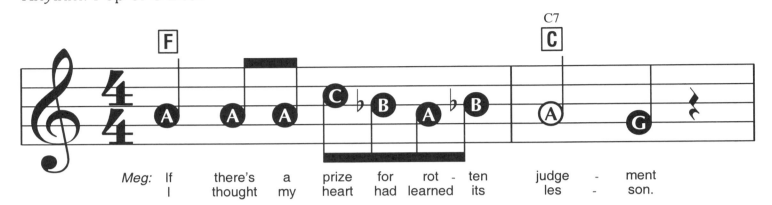

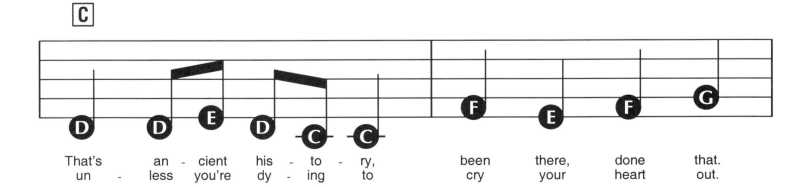

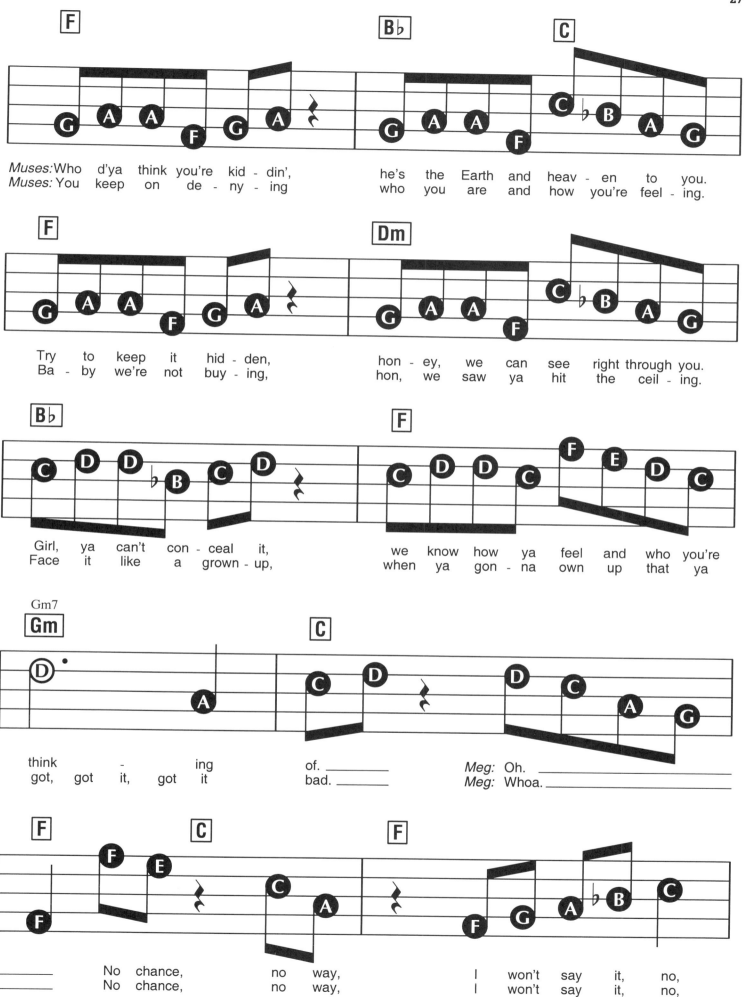

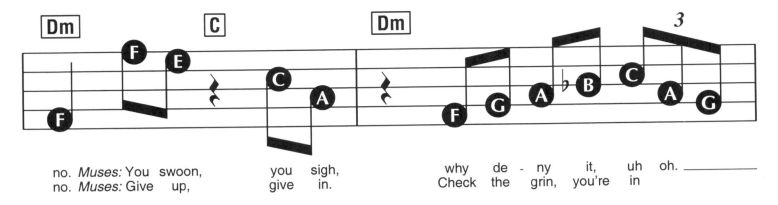

no. *Muses:* You swoon, you sigh, why de - ny it, uh oh. _____
no. *Muses:* Give up, give in. Check the grin, you're in

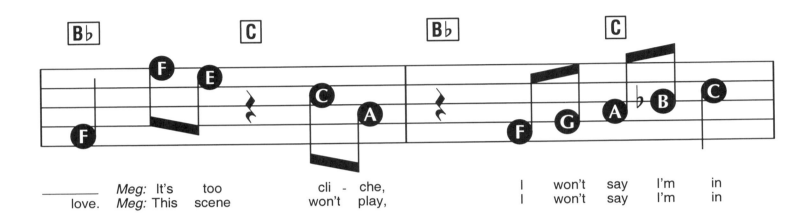

_____ *Meg:* It's too cli - che, I won't say I'm in
love. *Meg:* This scene won't play, I won't say I'm in

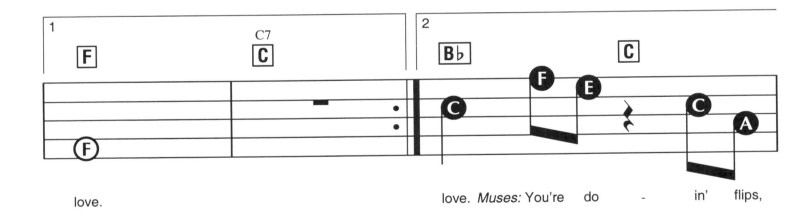

love. love. *Muses:* You're do - in' flips,

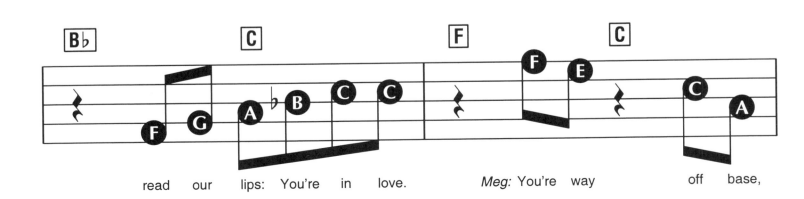

read our lips: You're in love. *Meg:* You're way off base,

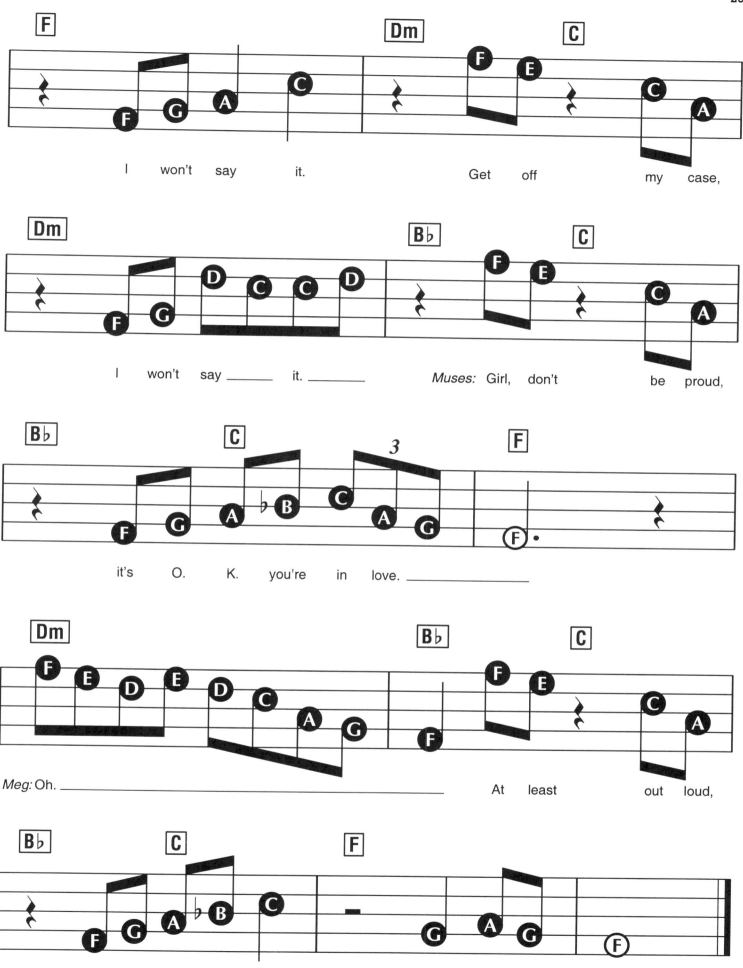

Forget About Love
from Walt Disney's THE RETURN OF JAFAR

Words and Music by Michael Silversher
and Patty Silversher

Registration 8
Rhythm: Shuffle

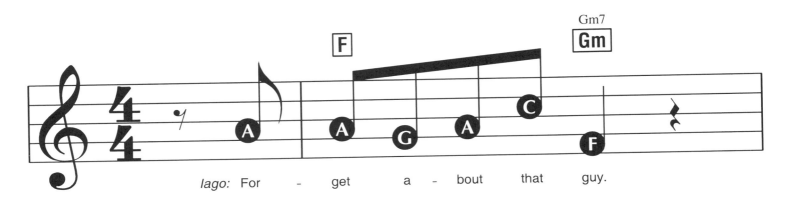

Iago: For - get a - bout that guy.

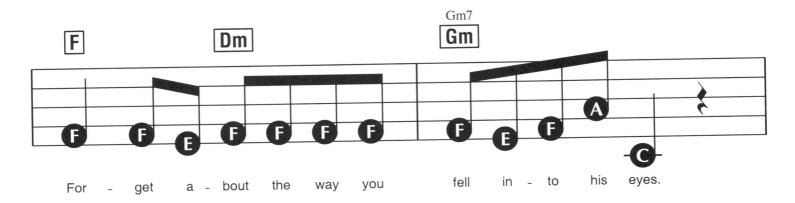

For - get a - bout the way you fell in - to his eyes.

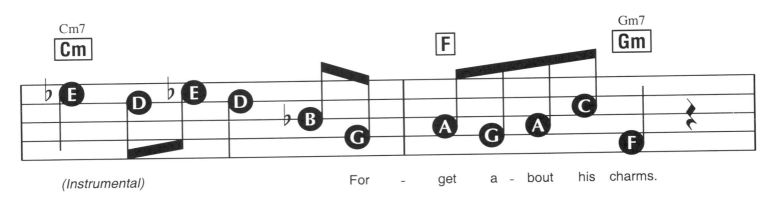

(Instrumental)　　　　For - get a - bout his charms.

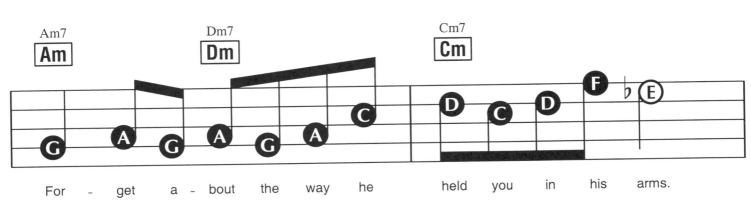

For - get a - bout the way he held you in his arms.

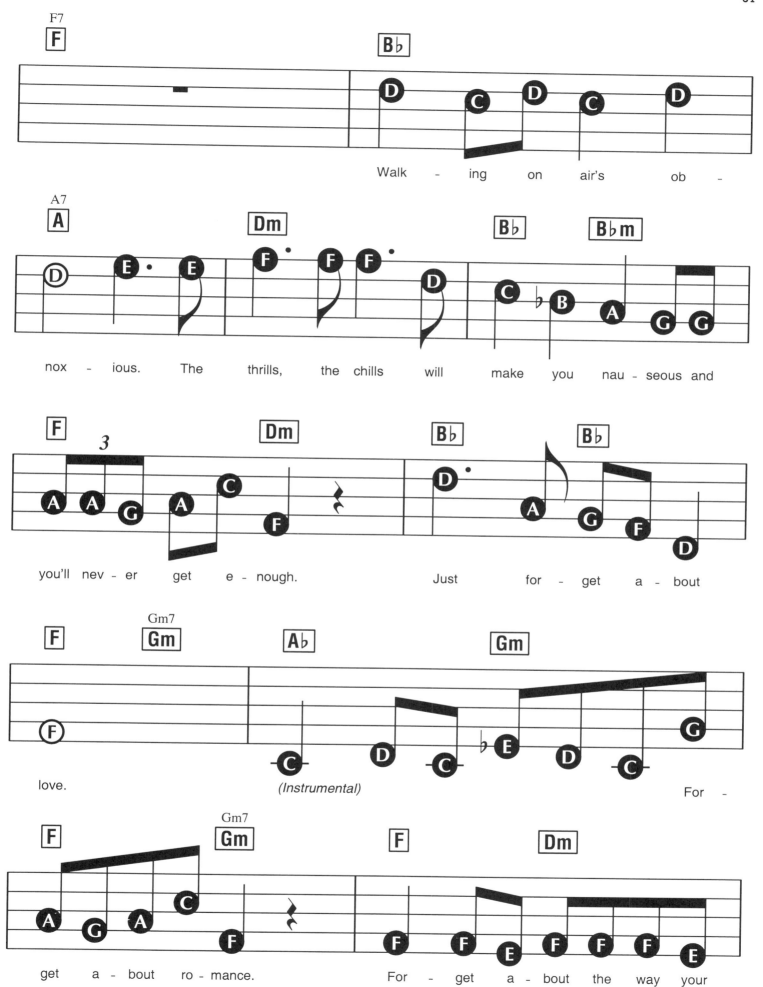

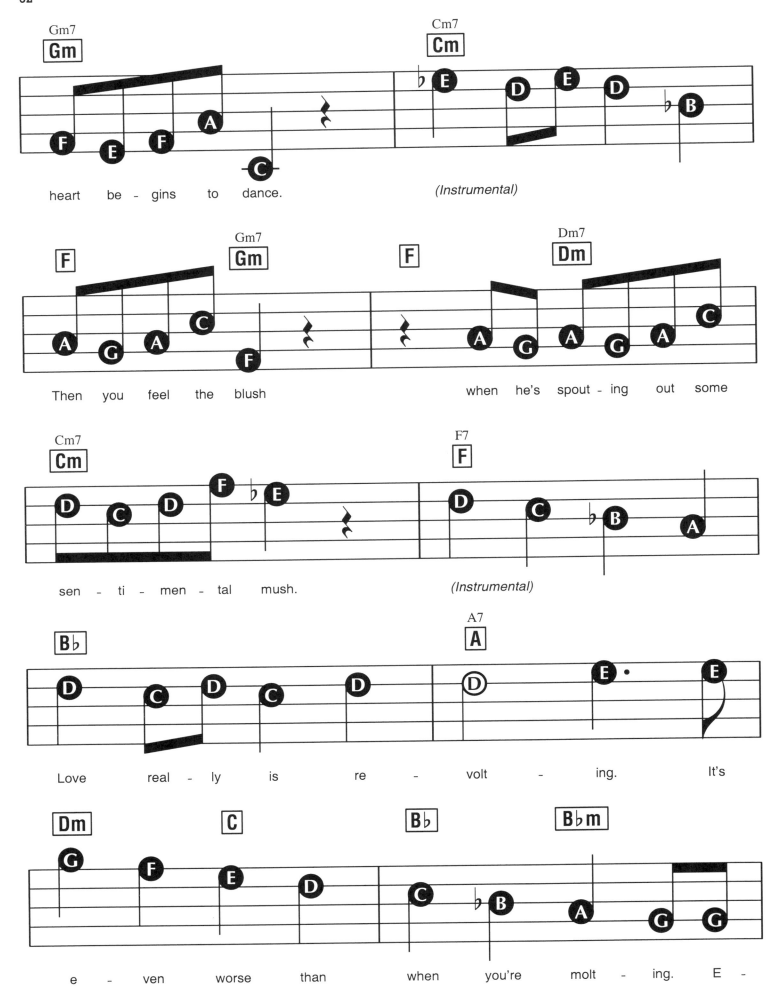

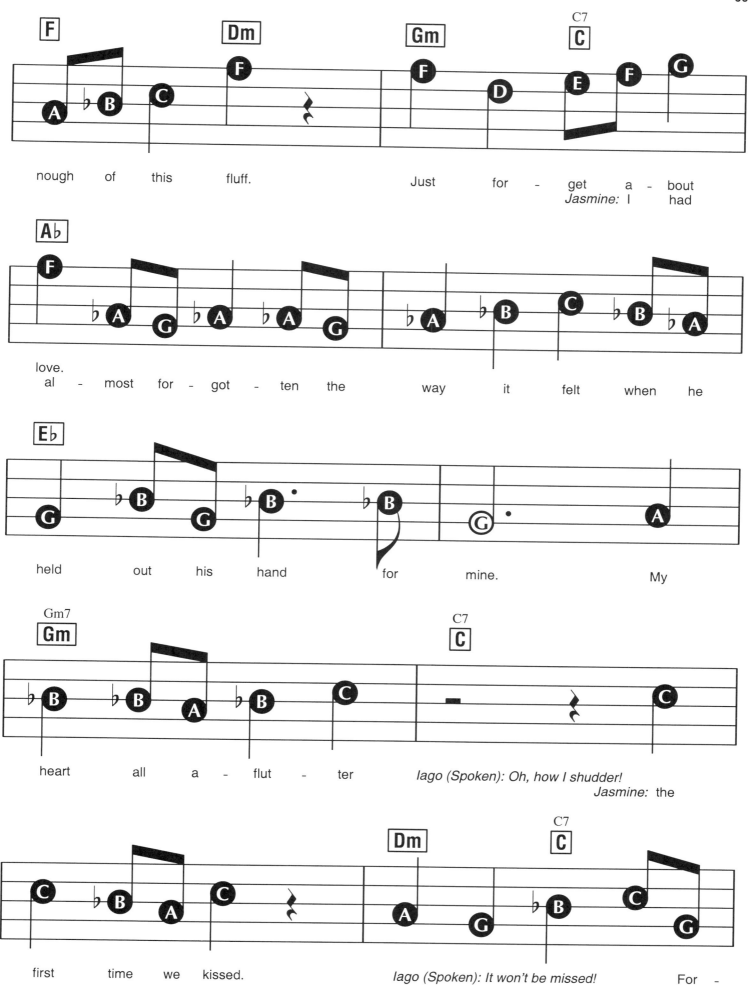

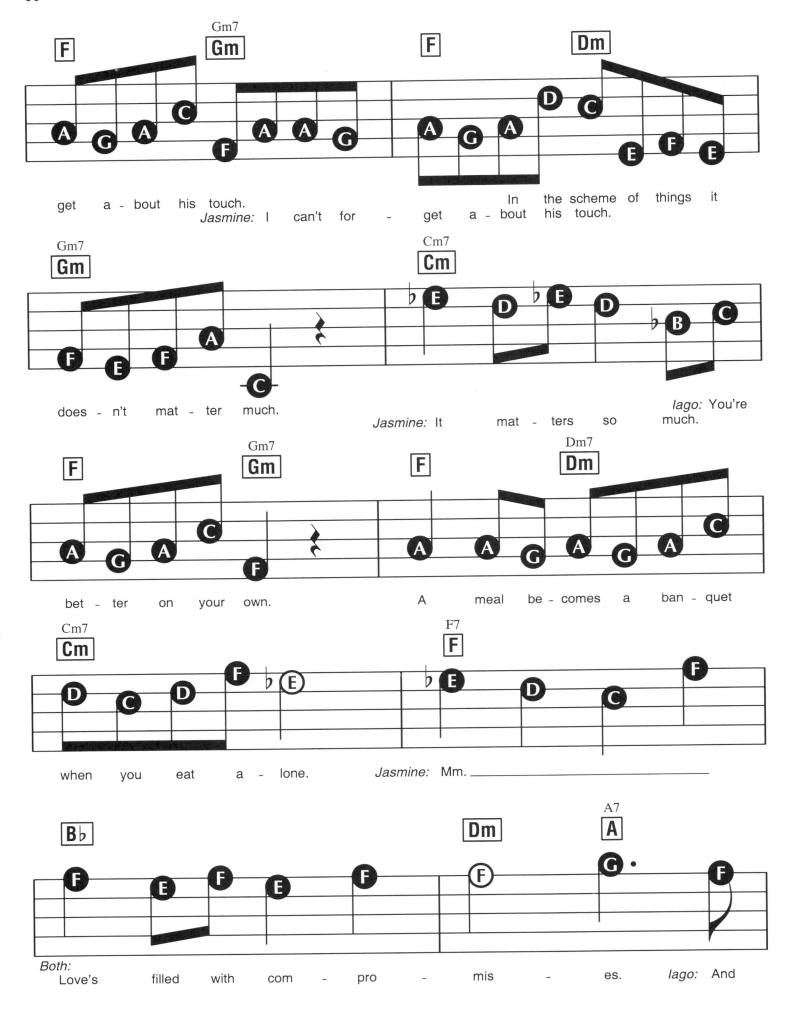

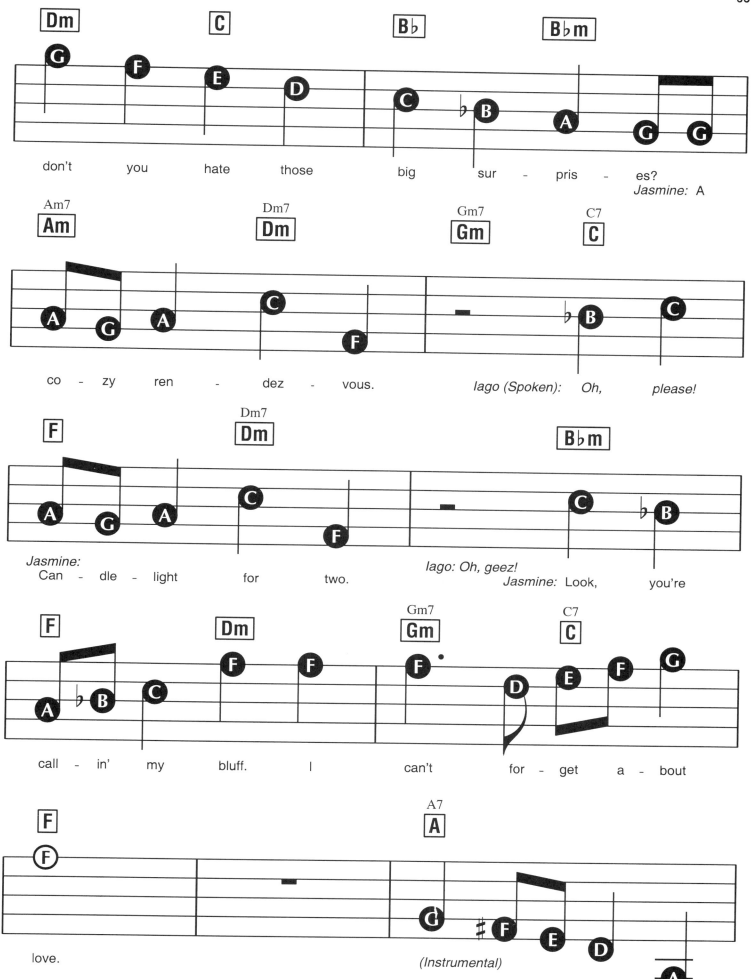

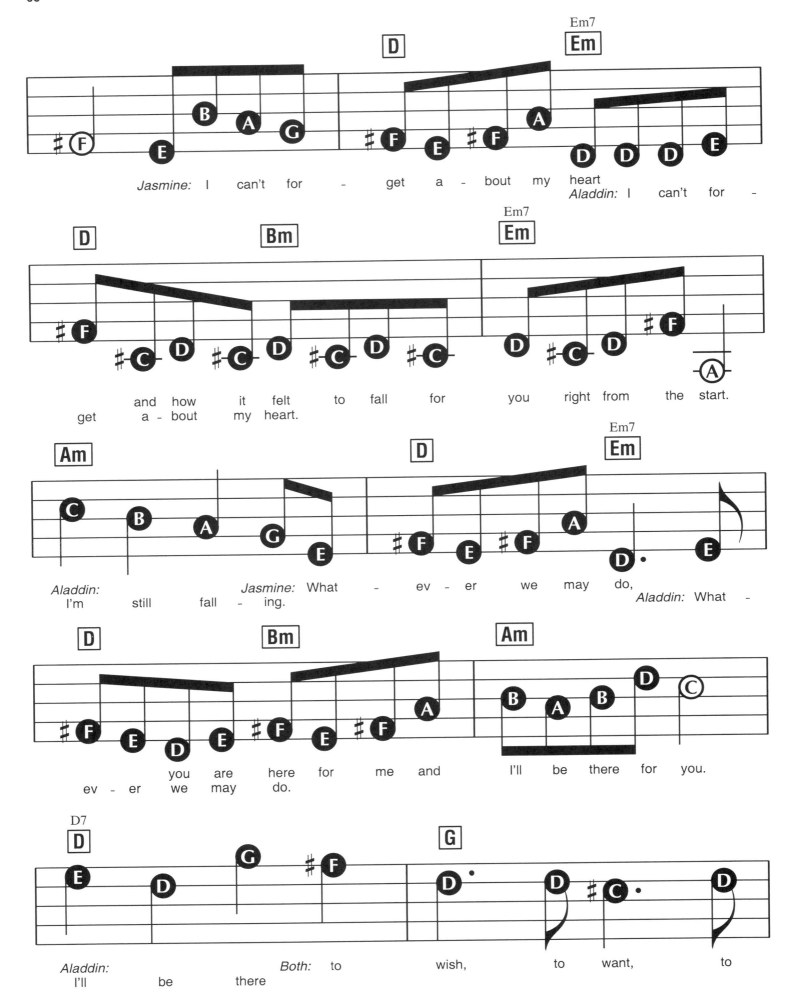

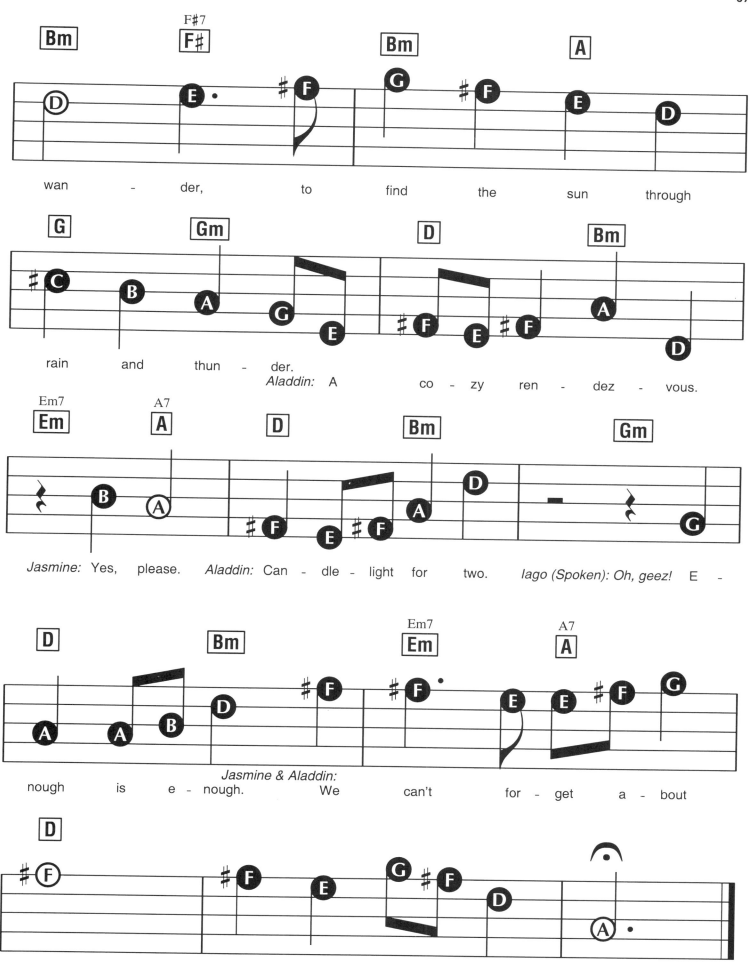

FORGET ABOUT LOVE

(The Return of Jafar)
Words and Music by Michael Silversher and Patty Silversher

Iago
Forget about that guy.
Forget about the way you fell into his eyes.
Forget about his charms.
Forget about the way he held you in his arms.
Walking on air's obnoxious.
The thrills, the chills will make you nauseous
And you'll never get enough.
Just forget about love.

Forget about romance.
Forget about the way your heart begins to dance.
Then you feel the blush
When he's spouting out some sentimental mush.

Love really is revolting.
It's even worse than when you're molting.
Enough of this fluff.
Just forget about love.

Jasmine
I had almost forgotten the way it felt
When he held out his hand for mine.
My heart all a–flutter
(Iago: Oh, how I shudder!)
The first time we kissed.
(Iago: It won't be missed!)

Iago
Forget about his touch.
(Jasmine: I can't forget about his touch.)
In the scheme of things it doesn't matter much.
(Jasmine: It matters so much.)
You're better on your own.
A meal becomes a banquet when you eat alone.
(Jasmine: Mm.)

Jasmine & Iago
Love's filled with compromises.

Iago
And don't you hate those big surprises?

Jasmine
A cozy rendezvous.
(Iago: Oh, please!)
Candlelight for two.
(Iago: Oh, geez!)
Look, you're callin' my bluff.
I can't forget about love.

I can't forget about my heart
(Aladdin: I can't forget about my heart.)
And how it felt to fall for you right from the start.
(Aladdin: I'm still falling.)
Whatever we may do,
(Aladdin: Whatever we may do.)
You are here for me and I'll be there for you.
(Aladdin: I'll be there)

Both
To wish, to want, to wander,
To find the sun through rain and thunder.

Aladdin
A cozy rendezvous.
(Jasmine: Yes, please.)
Candlelight for two.
(Iago: Oh, geez!)

Iago
Enough is enough.

Jasmine & Aladdin
We can't forget about love.

HOME
(Beauty and the Beast: The Broadway Musical)
Music by Alan Menken
Lyrics by Tim Rice

Yes, I made the choice.
For Papa, I will stay.
But I don't deserve to lose my freedom in this way,
You monster!
If you think that what you've done is right, well then
You're a fool!
Think again!

Is this home?
Is this where I should learn to be happy?
Never dreamed
That a home could be dark and cold.
I was told
Ev'ry day in my childhood:
Even when we grow old,
Home will be where the heart is.
Never were words so true!
My heart's far, far away.
Home is too.

Is this home?
Is this what I must learn to believe in?
Try to find
Something good in this tragic place.
Just in case
I should stay here forever
Held in this empty space.
Oh, but that won't be easy.
I know the reason why:
My heart's far, far away.
Home's a lie.

What I'd give to return
To the life that I knew lately.
And to think I complained
Of that dull provincial town.

Is this home?
Am I here for a day or forever?
Shut away
From the world until who knows when,
Oh, but then,
As my life has been altered once,
It can change again.
Build higher walls around me,
Change ev'ry lock and key.

Nothing lasts,
Nothing holds
All of me.
My heart's far, far away,
Home and free!

Home
from Walt Disney's BEAUTY AND THE BEAST:
THE BROADWAY MUSICAL

Registration 8
Rhythm: 4/4 Ballad or Fox Trot

Music by Alan Menken
Lyrics by Tim Rice

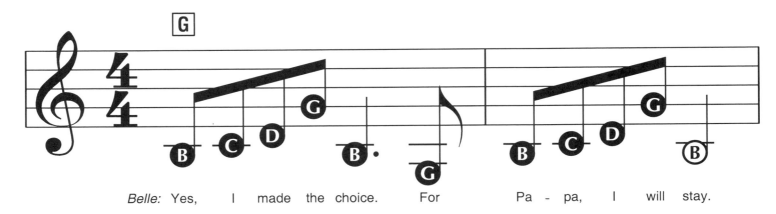

Belle: Yes, I made the choice. For Pa - pa, I will stay.

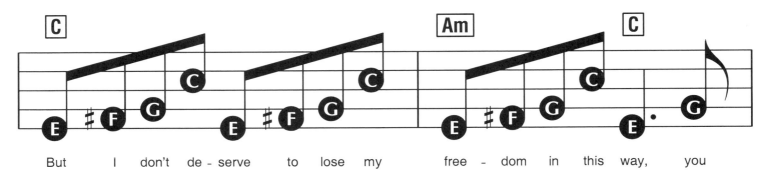

But I don't de - serve to lose my free - dom in this way, you

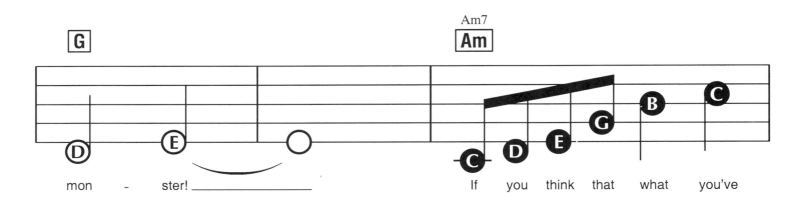

mon - ster! _____ If you think that what you've

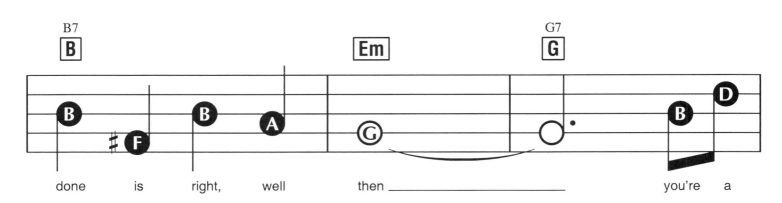

done is right, well then _____ you're a

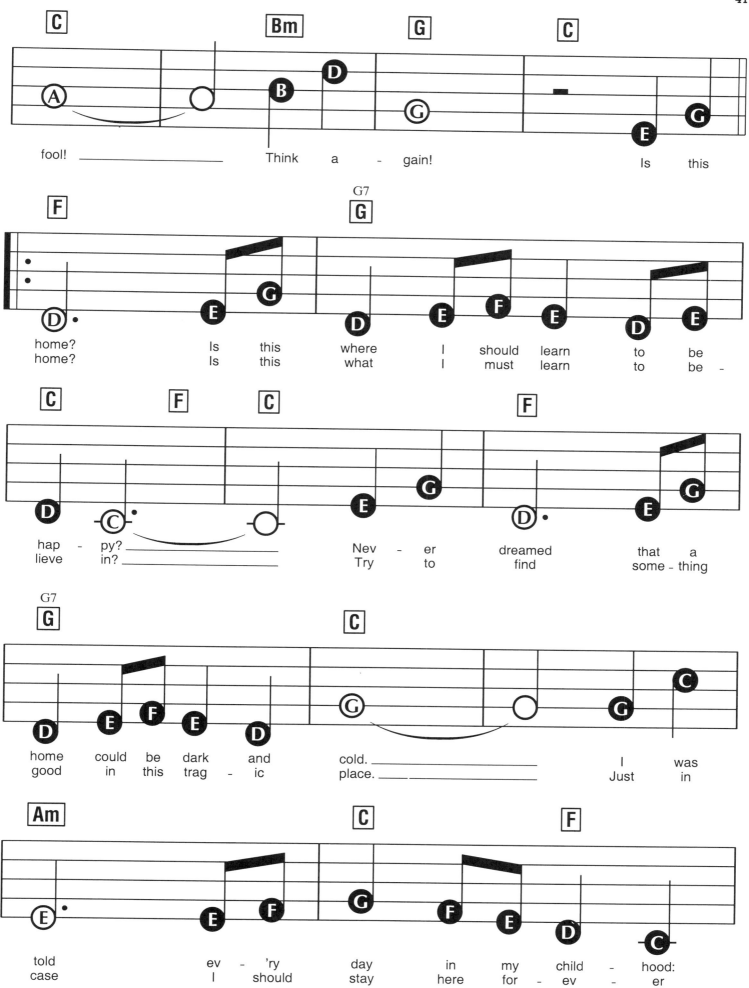

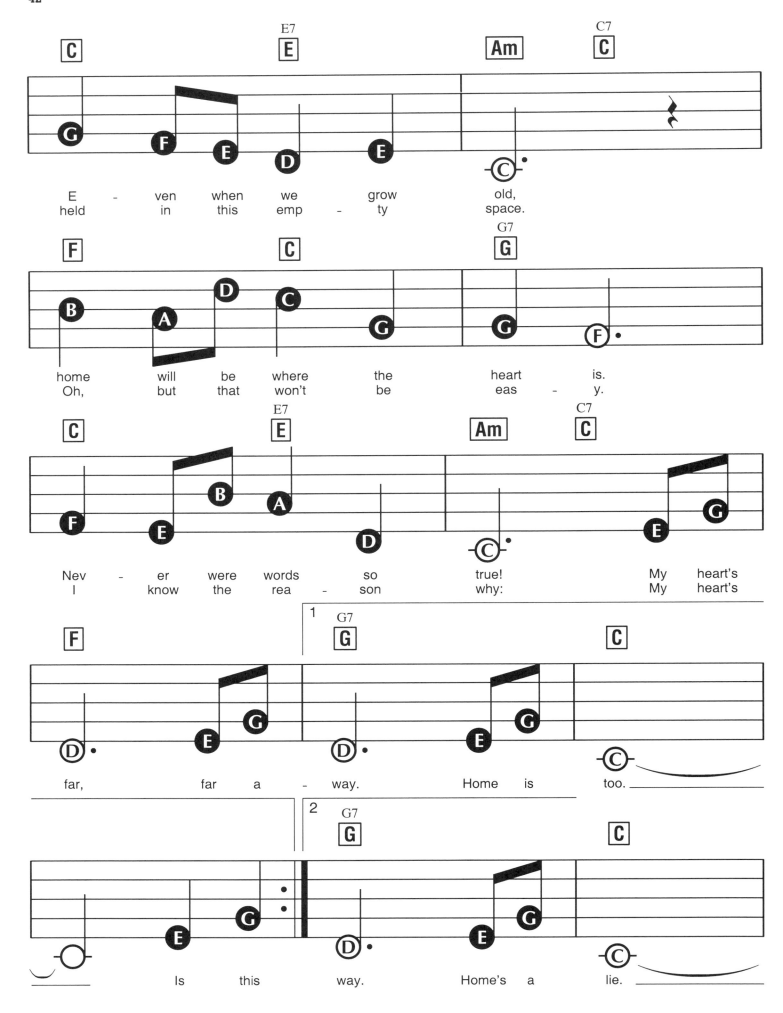

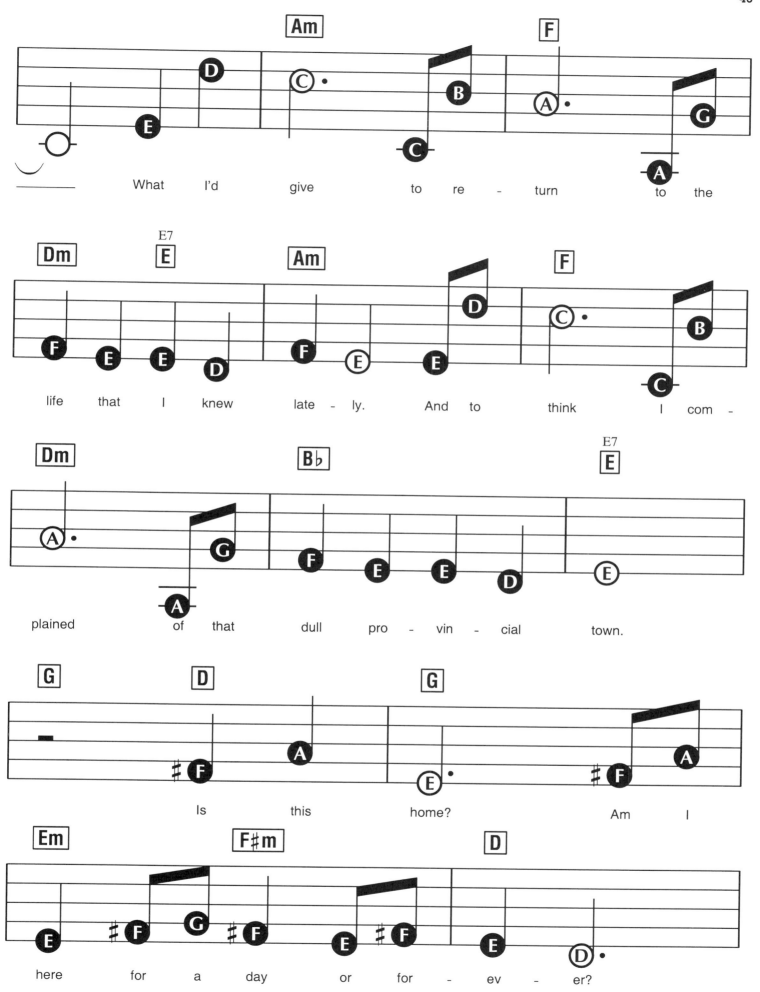

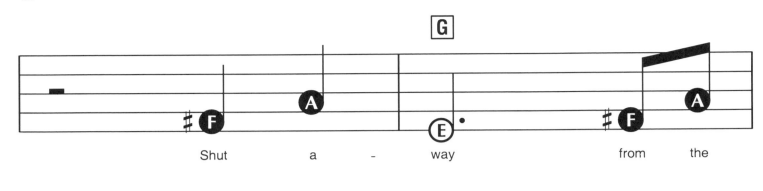

Shut a - way from the

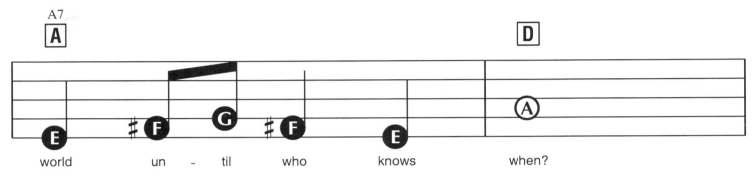

world un - til who knows when?

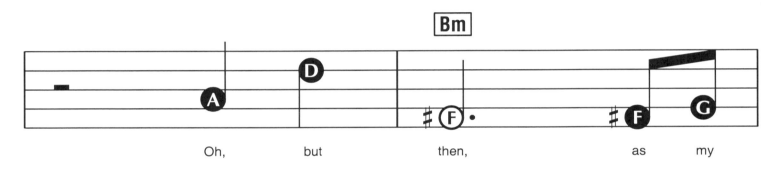

Oh, but then, as my

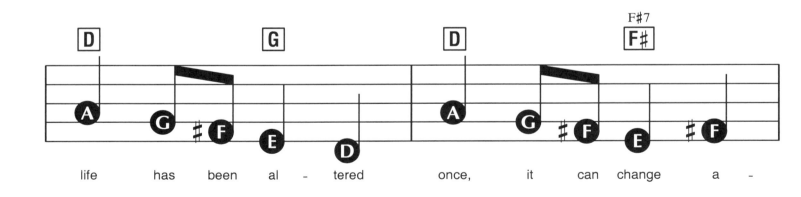

life has been al - tered once, it can change a -

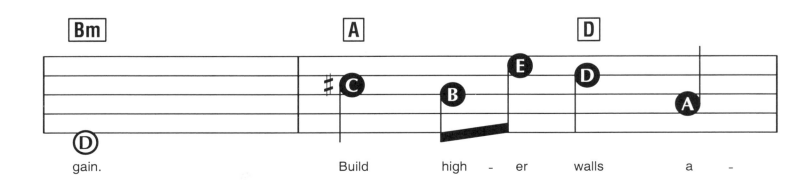

gain. Build high - er walls a -

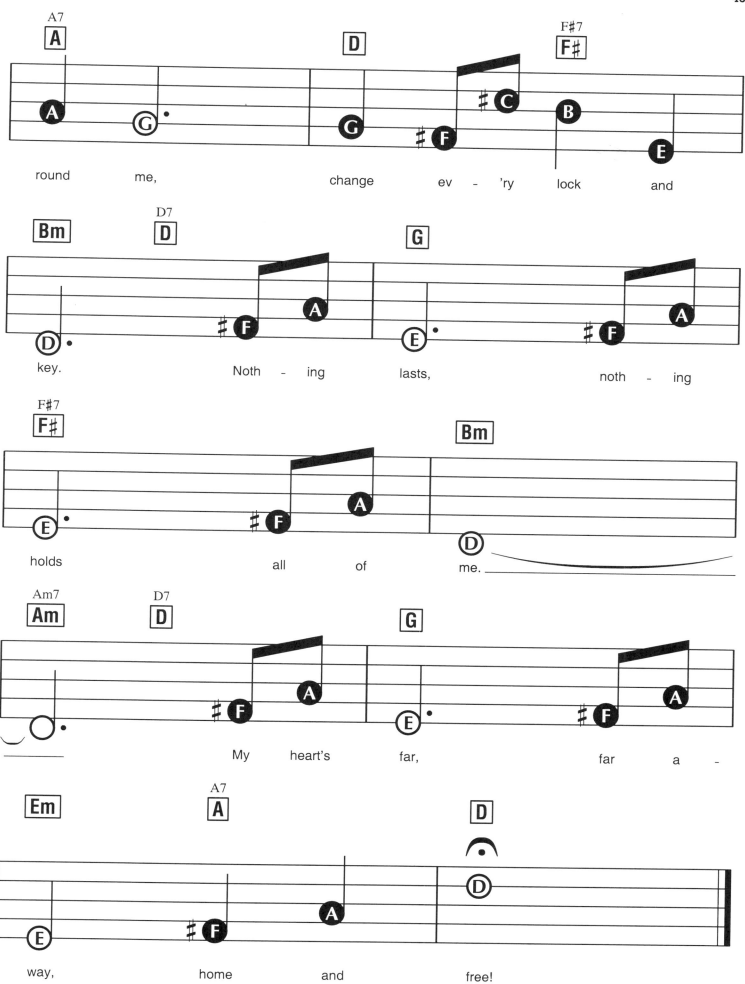

I Wonder
from Walt Disney's SLEEPING BEAUTY

Words by Winston Hibler and Ted Sears
Music by George Bruns
Adapted from a Theme by Tchaikovsky

Registration 1
Rhythm: Waltz

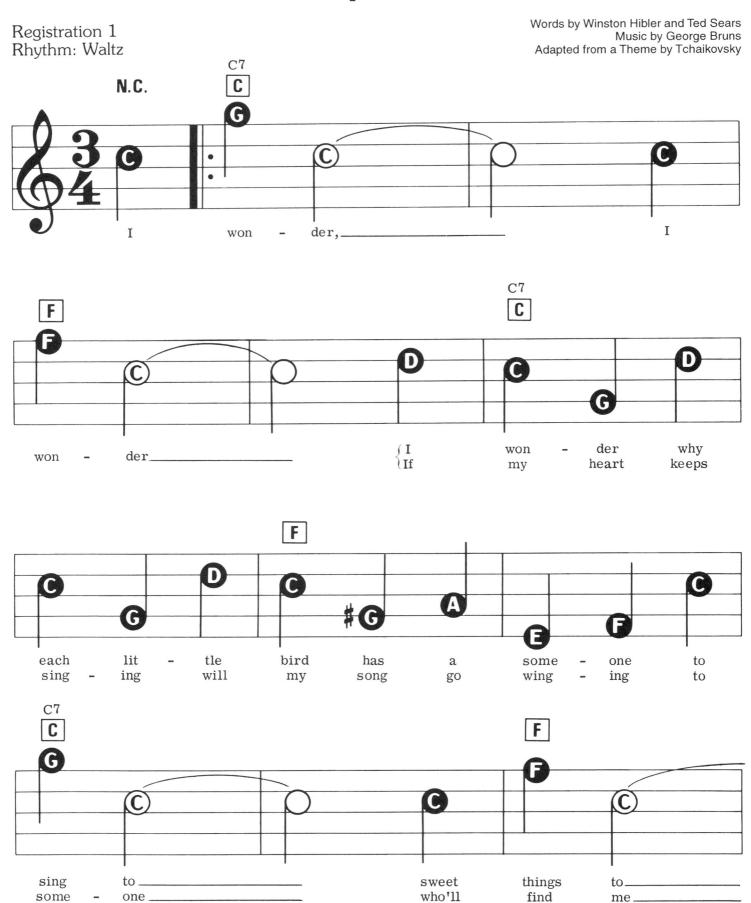

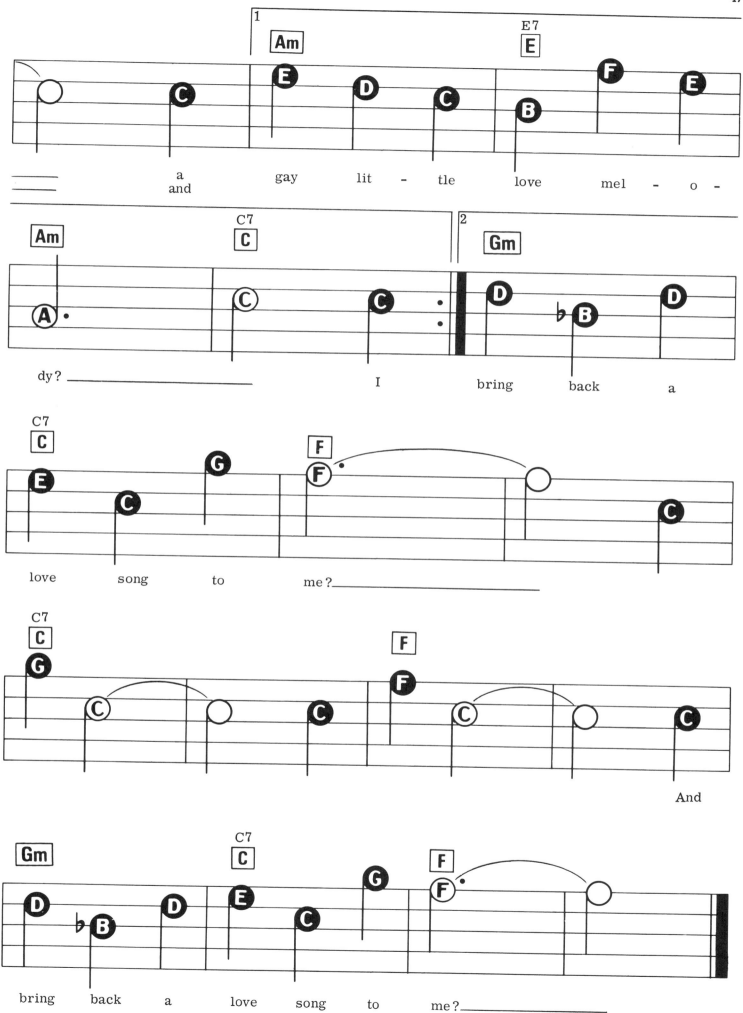

Love
from Walt Disney's ROBIN HOOD

Registration 2
Rhythm: Fox Trot or Swing

Words by Floyd Huddleston
Music by George Bruns

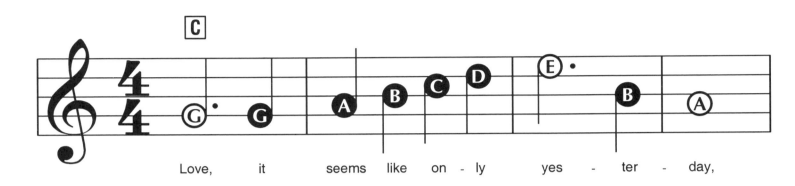

Love, it seems like on - ly yes - ter - day,

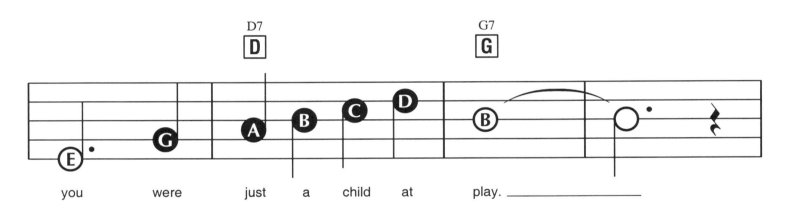

you were just a child at play. _____

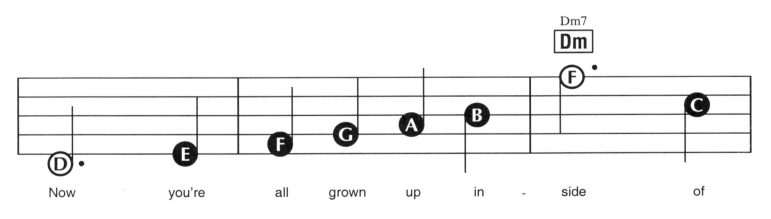

Now you're all grown up in - side of

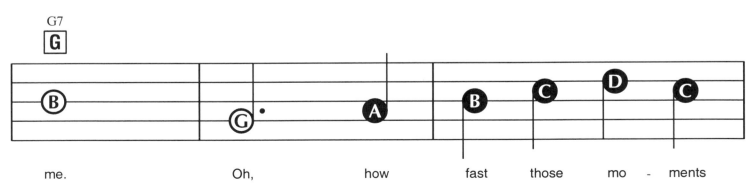

me. Oh, how fast those mo - ments

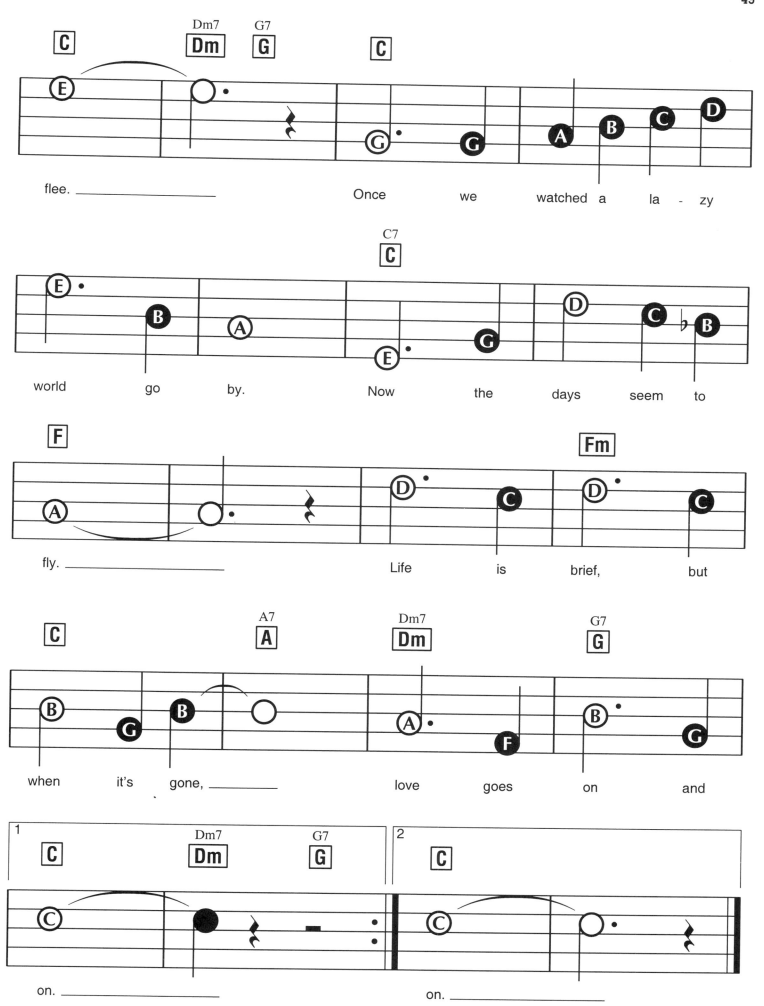

I WONDER
(Sleeping Beauty)
Words by Winston Hibler and Ted Sears
Music by George Bruns
Adapted from a Theme by Tchaikovsky

I wonder, I wonder,
I wonder why each little bird has a someone
To sing to,
Sweet things to,
A gay little love melody?
I wonder, I wonder,
If my heart keeps singing will my song go winging
To someone
Who'll find me
And bring back a love song to me?

LOVE
(Robin Hood)
Words by Floyd Huddleston
Music by George Bruns

Love, it seems like only yesterday,
You were just a child at play.
Now you're all grown up inside of me.
Oh, how fast those moments flee.

Once we watched a lazy world go by.
Now the days seem to fly.
Life is brief, but when it's gone,
Love goes on and on.

Love will live, love will last.
Love goes on and on and on.

Once we watched a lazy world go by.
Now the days seem to fly.
Life is brief, but when it's gone,
Love goes on and on.

IF I CAN'T LOVE HER
(Beauty and the Beast: The Broadway Musical)
Music by Alan Menken
Lyrics by Tim Rice

And in my twisted face
There's not the slightest trace
Of anything that even hints at kindness.
And from my tortured shape,
No comfort, no escape.
I see, but deep within is utter blindness.

Hopeless,
As my dream dies.
As the time flies,
Love a lost illusion.
Helpless,
Unforgiven.
Cold and driven
To this sad conclusion.

No beauty could move me,
No goodness improve me.
No power on Earth, if I can't love her.
No passion could reach me,
No lesson could teach me
How I could have loved her and make her love me too.
If I can't love her, then who?

Long ago, I should have seen
All the things I could have been.
Careless and unthinking, I moved onward!

No pain could be deeper.
No life could be cheaper.
No point anymore, if I can't love her.
No spirit could win me.
No hope left within me,
Hope I could have loved her and that she'd set me free.
But it's not to be.
If I can't love her,
Let the world be done with me.

If I Can't Love Her
from Walt Disney's BEAUTY AND THE BEAST: THE BROADWAY MUSICAL

Registration 8
Rhythm: 4/4 Ballad or Fox Trot

Music by Alan Menken
Lyrics by Tim Rice

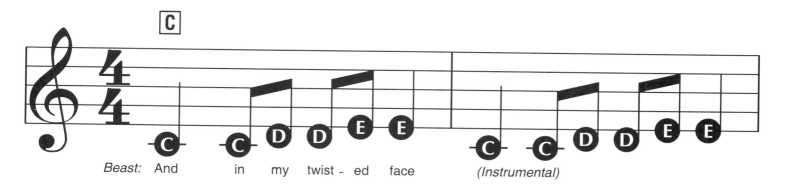

Beast: And in my twist - ed face   (Instrumental)

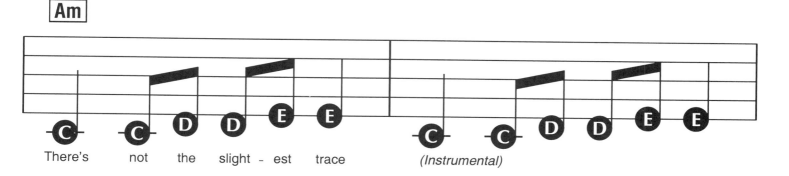

There's not the slight - est trace   (Instrumental)

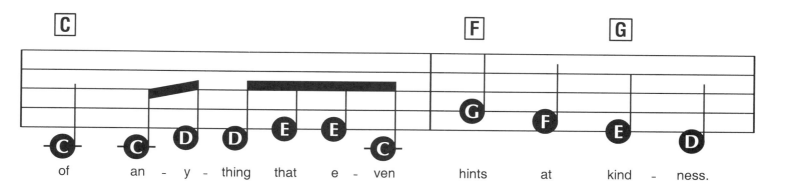

of an - y - thing that e - ven hints at kind - ness.

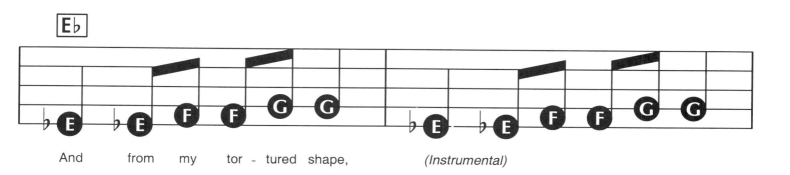

And from my tor - tured shape,   (Instrumental)

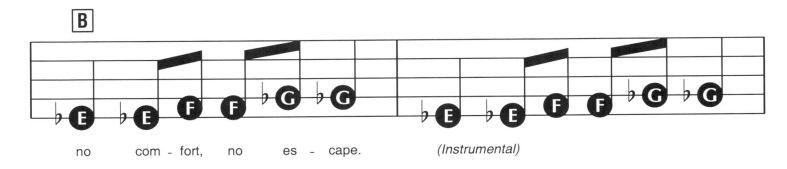

no com - fort, no es - cape. *(Instrumental)*

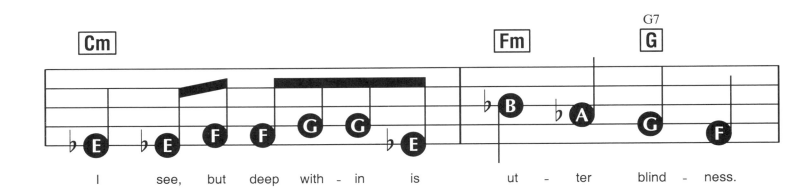

I see, but deep with - in is ut - ter blind - ness.

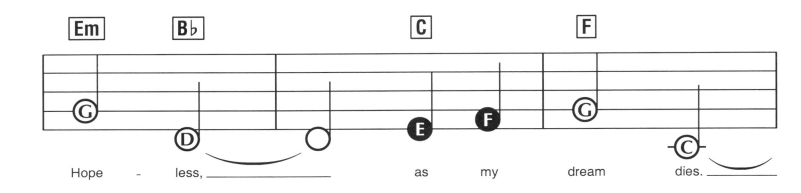

Hope - less, _____ as my dream dies. _____

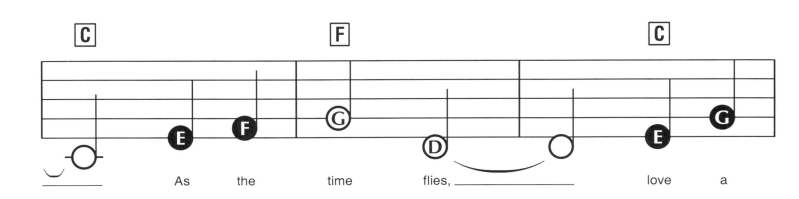

_____ As the time flies, _____ love a

53

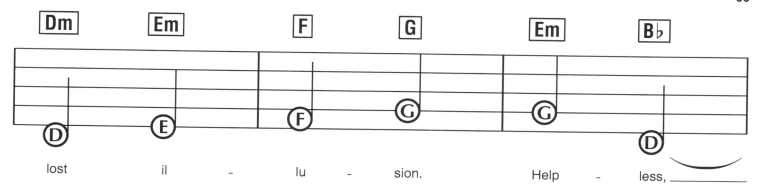

lost il - lu - sion. Help - less,

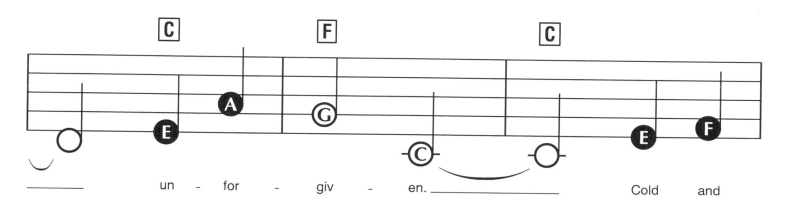

un - for - giv - en. Cold and

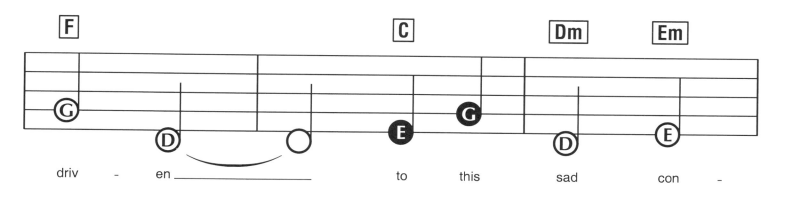

driv - en to this sad con -

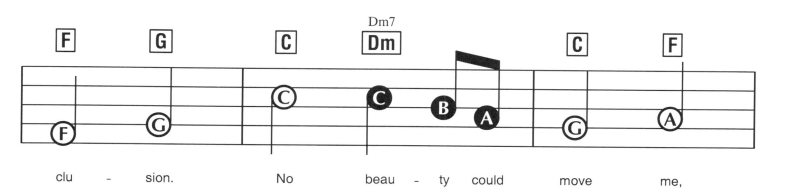

clu - sion. No beau - ty could move me,

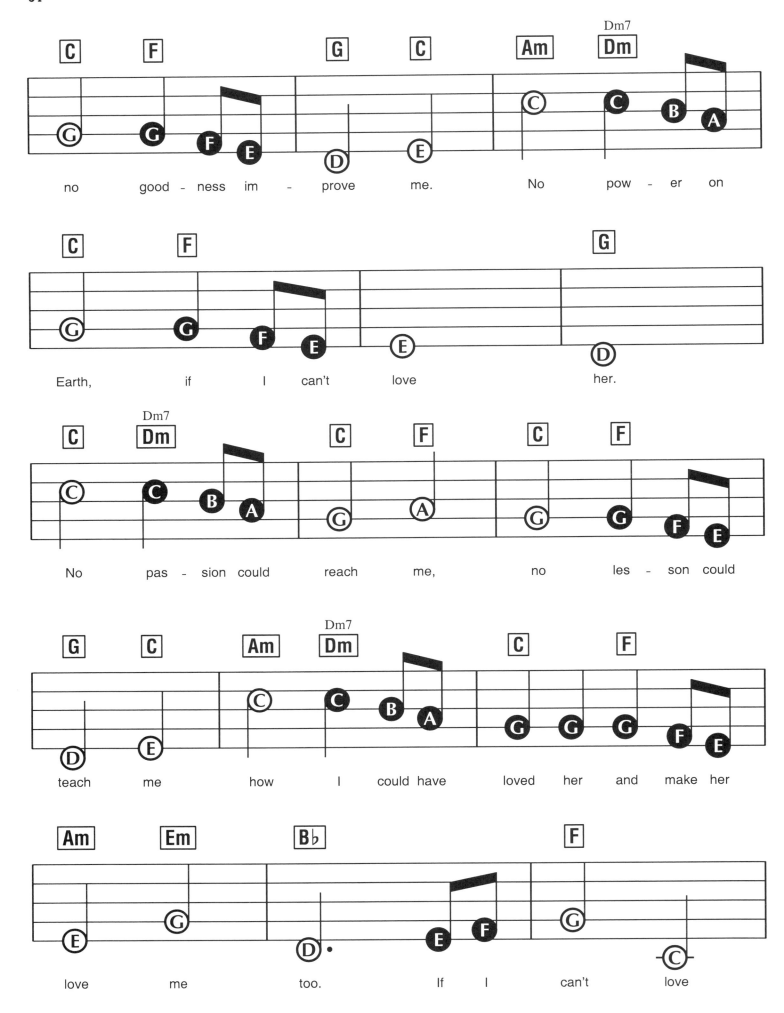

55

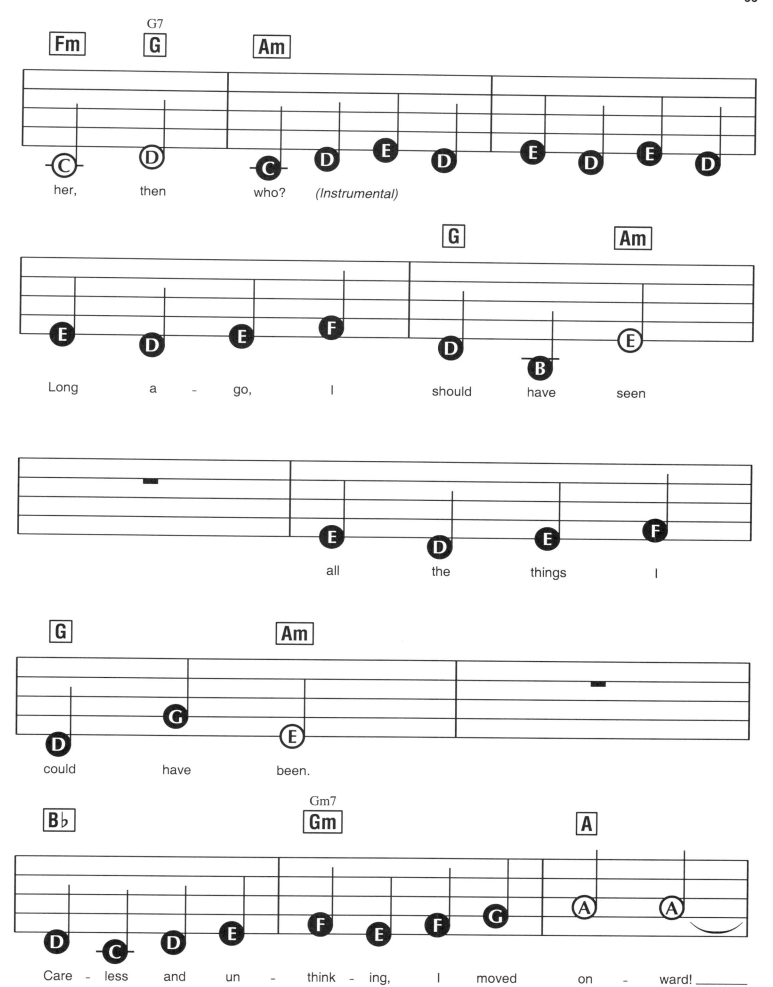

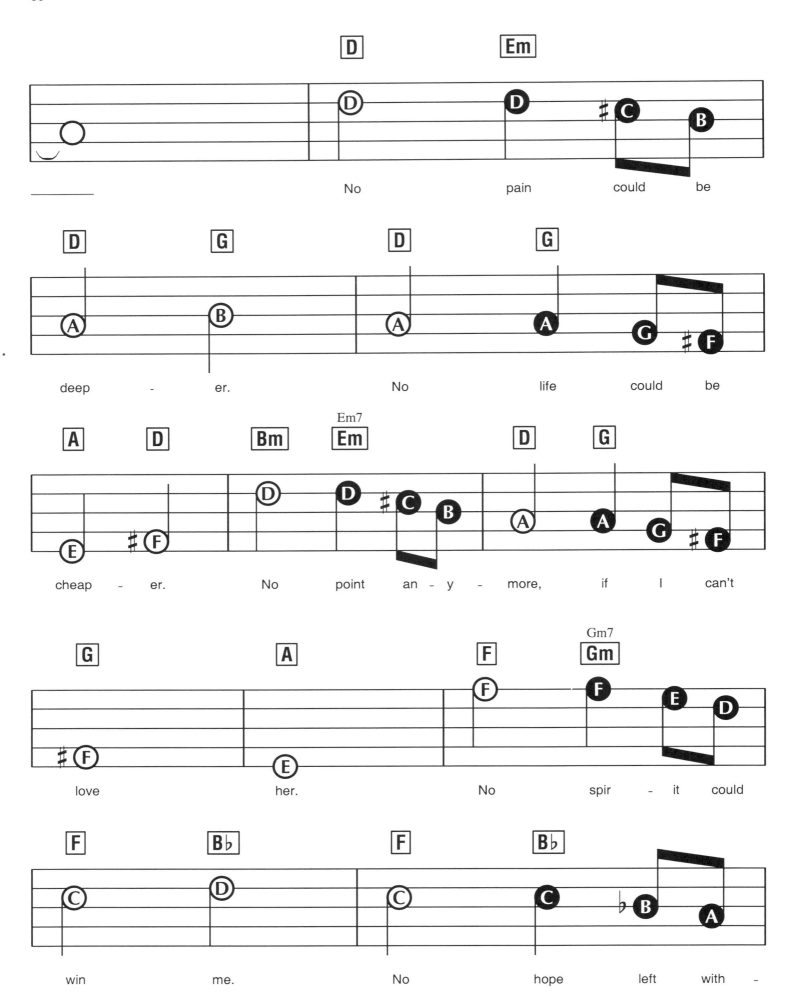

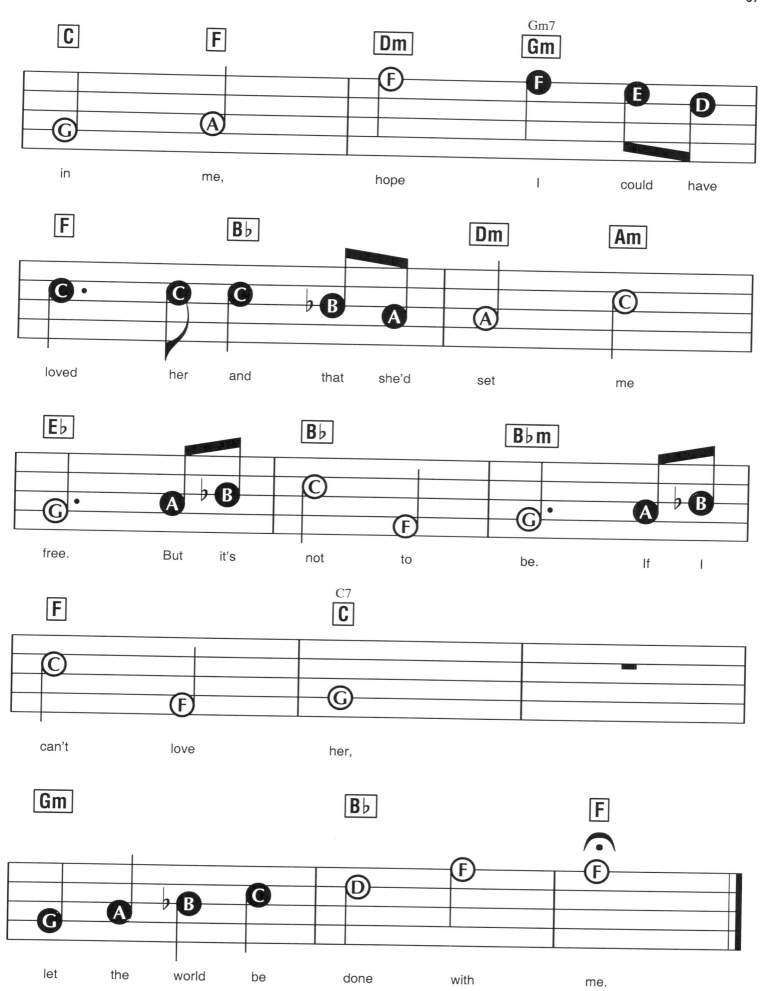

JUST AROUND THE RIVERBEND

(Pocahontas)
Music by Alan Menken
Lyrics by Stephen Schwartz

What I love most about rivers is:
You can't step in the same river twice.
The water's always changing, always flowing.
But people, I guess, can't live like that;
We all must pay a price:
To be safe we lose our chance of ever knowing
What's around the riverbend,
Waiting just around the riverbend.

I look once more
Just around the riverbend
Beyond the shore,
Where the gulls fly free.
Don't know what for,
What I dream the day might send
Just around the riverbend
For me,
Coming for me.

I feel it there beyond those trees
Or right behind these waterfalls.
Can I ignore the sound of distant drumming
For a handsome sturdy husband
Who builds handsome sturdy walls
And never dreams that something might be coming
Just around the riverbend?
Just around the riverbend.

I look once more
Just around the riverbend
Beyond the shore,
Somewhere past the sea.
Don't know what for...
Why do all my dreams extend
Just around the riverbend?
Just around the riverbend.

Should I choose the smoothest course
Steady as the beating drum?
Should I marry Kocoum?
Is all my dreaming at an end?
Or do you still wait for me, Dream Giver
Just around the riverbend?

Just Around the Riverbend
from Walt Disney's POCAHONTAS

Registration 2
Rhythm: 8-Beat

Music by Alan Menken
Lyrics by Stephen Schwartz

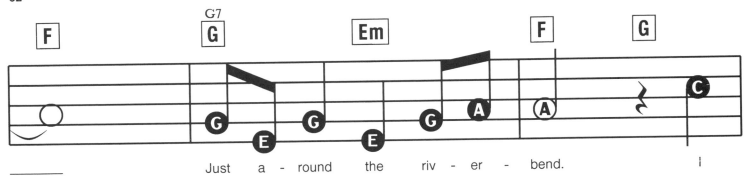

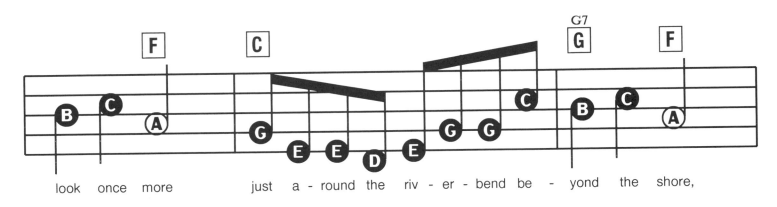

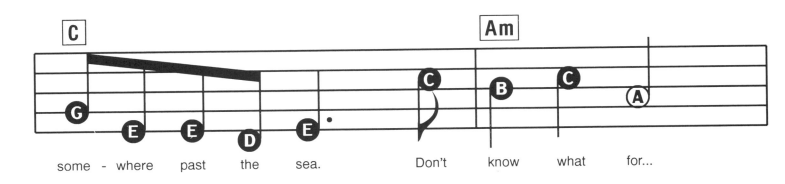

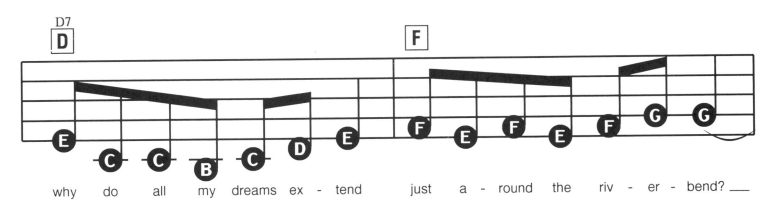

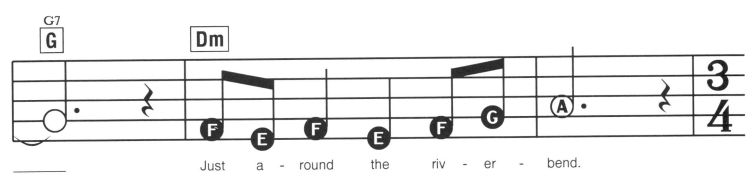

63

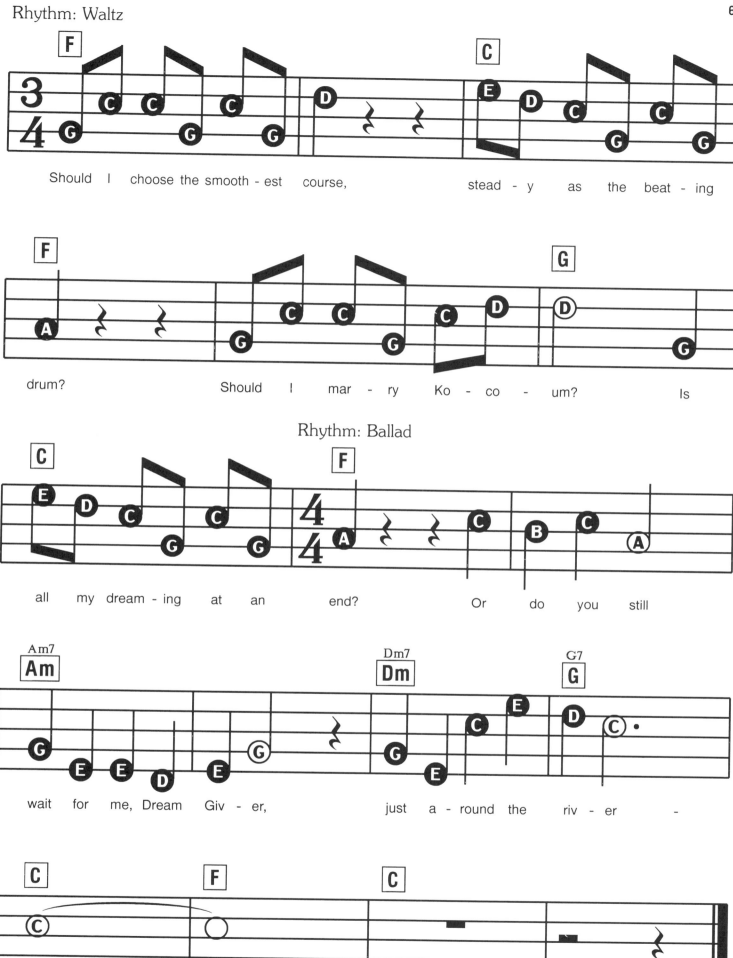

Once Upon a Dream
from Walt Disney's SLEEPING BEAUTY

Registration 2
Rhythm: Waltz

Words and Music by Sammy Fain and Jack Lawrence
Adapted from a Theme by Tchaikovsky

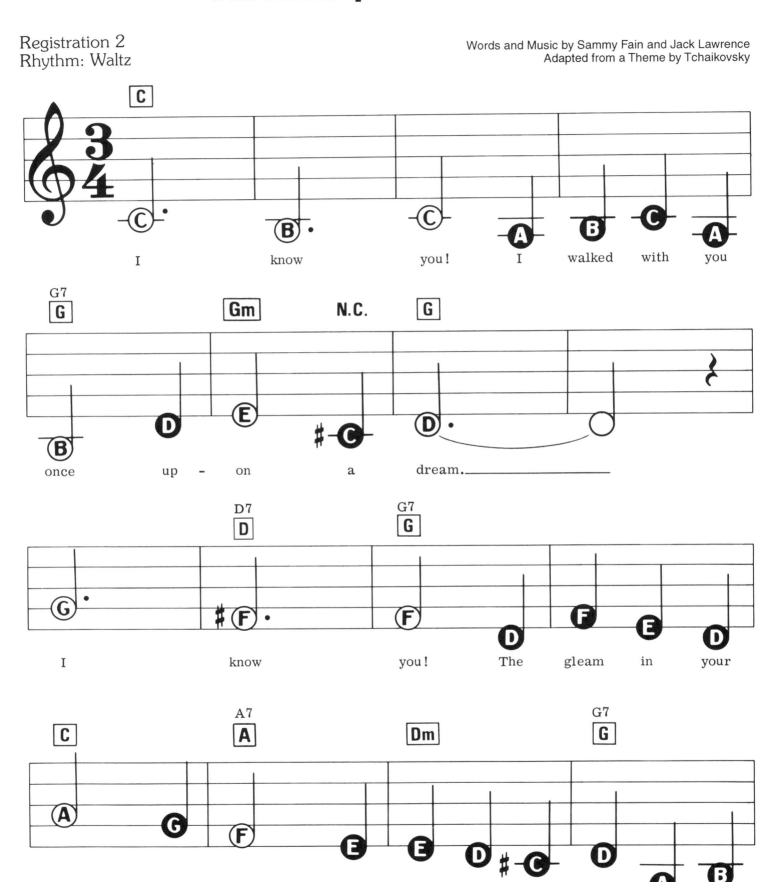

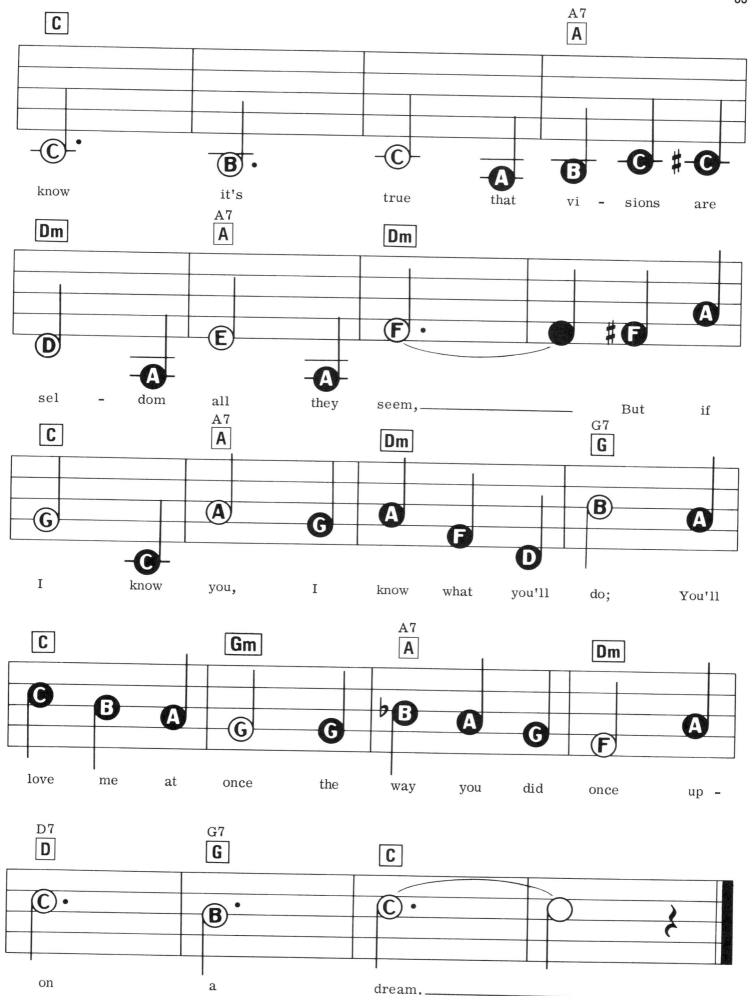

ONCE UPON A DREAM

(Sleeping Beauty)
Words and Music by Sammy Fain and Jack Lawrence
Adapted from a Theme by Tchaikovsky

I know you!
I walked with you once upon a dream.
I know you!
The gleam in your eyes is so familiar a gleam.
Yet I know it's true that visions are seldom all they seem,
But if I know you,
I know what you'll do;
You'll love me at once
The way you did once upon a dream.

But if I know you,
I know what you'll do;
You'll love me at once
The way you did once upon a dream.

I know you!
I walked with you once upon a dream.
I know you!
The gleam in your eyes is so familiar a gleam.
And I know it's true that visions are seldom all they seem,
But if I know you,
I know what you'll do;
You'll love me at once
The way you did once upon a dream.

KISS THE GIRL

(The Little Mermaid)
Lyrics by Howard Ashman
Music by Alan Menken

There you see her,
Sitting there across the way.
She don't got a lot to say,
But there's something about her.
And you don't know why,
But you're dying to try.
You wanna kiss the girl.

Yes, you want her.
Look at her, you know you do.
Possible she wants you, too.
There is one way to ask her.
It don't take a word,
Not a single word,
Go on and kiss the girl.

Sha la la la la la, my oh my,
Look like the boy too shy.
Ain't gonna kiss the girl.
Sha la la la la la, ain't that sad.
Ain't it a shame, too bad.
He gonna miss the girl.

Now's your moment,
Floating in a blue lagoon.
Boy, you better do it soon,
No time will be better.
She don't say a word
And she won't say a word
Until you kiss the girl.

Sha la la la la la, don't be scared.
You got the mood prepared,
Go on and kiss the girl.
Sha la la la la la, don't stop now.
Don't try to hide it how
You wanna kiss the girl.

Sha la la la la la, float along
And listen to the song,
The song say kiss the girl.
Sha la la la la the music play.
Do what the music say.
You gotta kiss the girl.

You've got to kiss the girl.
You wanna kiss the girl.
You've gotta kiss the girl.
Go on and kiss the girl.

Kiss the Girl
from Walt Disney's THE LITTLE MERMAID

Registration 7
Rhythm: Bossa Nova or Latin

Lyrics by Howard Ashman
Music by Alan Menken

Yes, you want her. Look at her, you know you

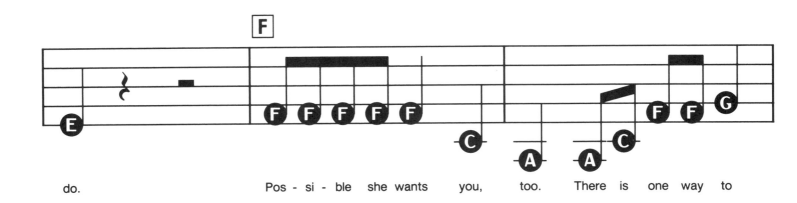

do. Pos - si - ble she wants you, too. There is one way to

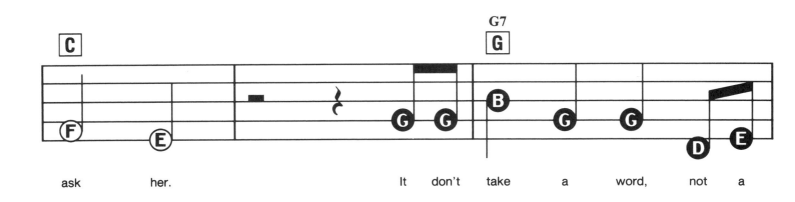

ask her. It don't take a word, not a

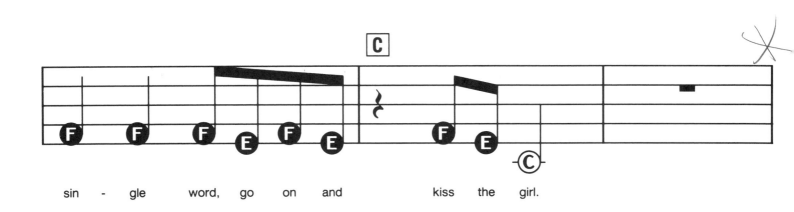

sin - gle word, go on and kiss the girl.

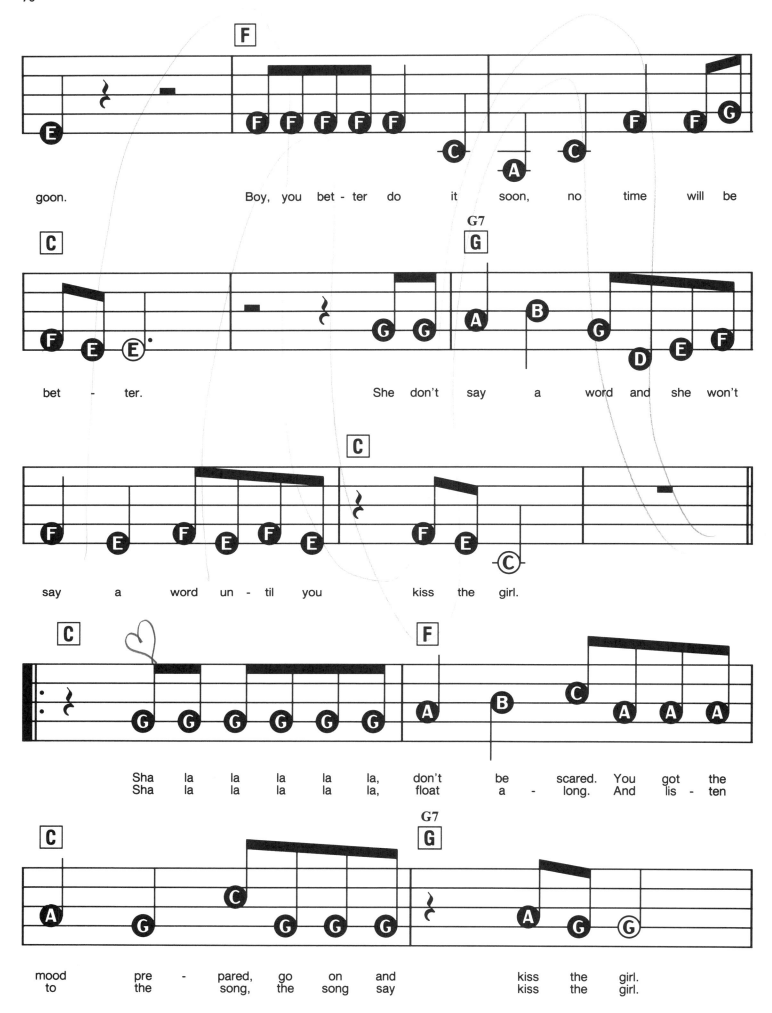

Out of Thin Air
from Walt Disney's ALADDIN AND THE KING OF THIEVES

Registration 8
Rhythm: Broadway

Words and Music by
David Friedman

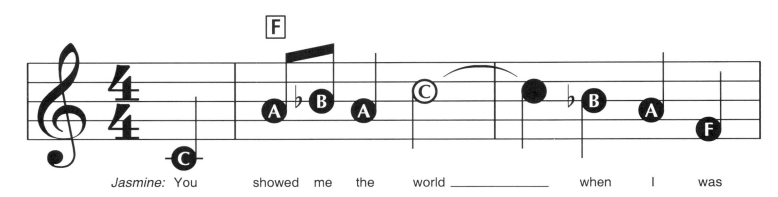

Jasmine: You   showed   me   the   world _____ when   I   was

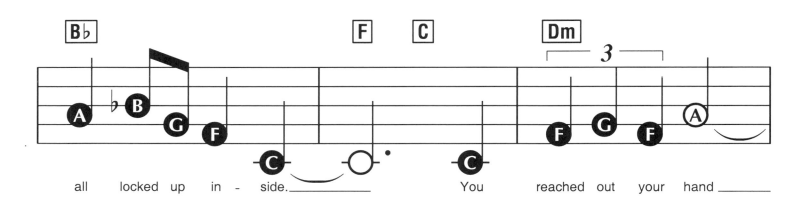

all   locked   up   in - side. _____   You   reached   out   your   hand _____

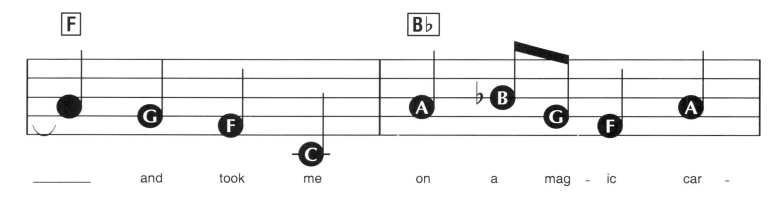

_____   and   took   me   on   a   mag - ic   car -

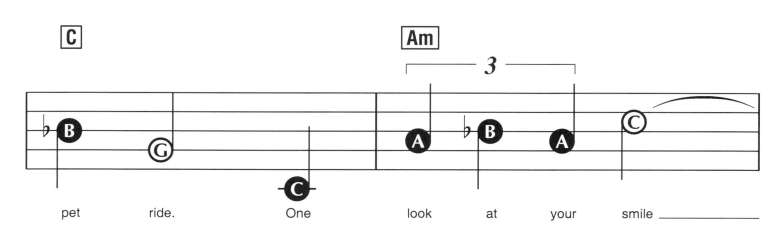

pet   ride.   One   look   at   your   smile _____

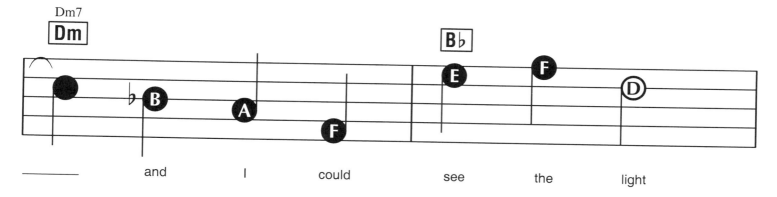

and   I   could   see   the   light

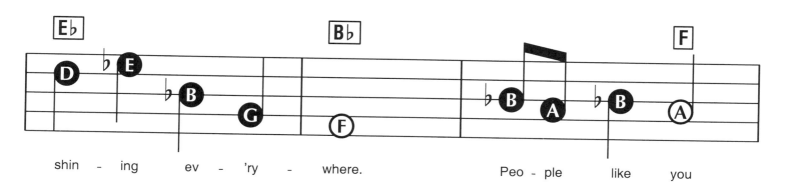

shin – ing   ev – 'ry – where.   Peo – ple   like   you

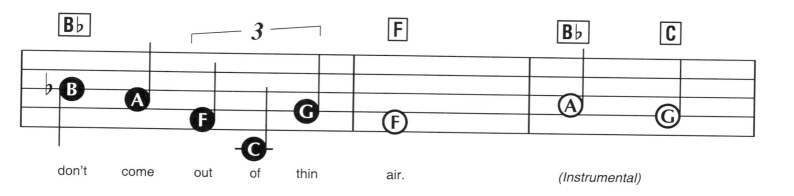

don't   come   out   of   thin   air.   (Instrumental)

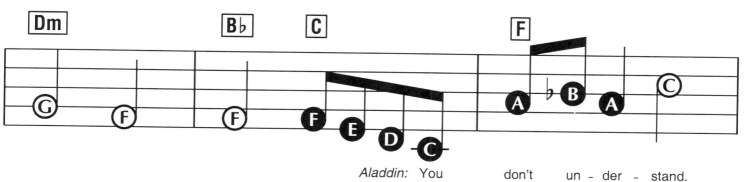

Aladdin: You   don't   un – der – stand.

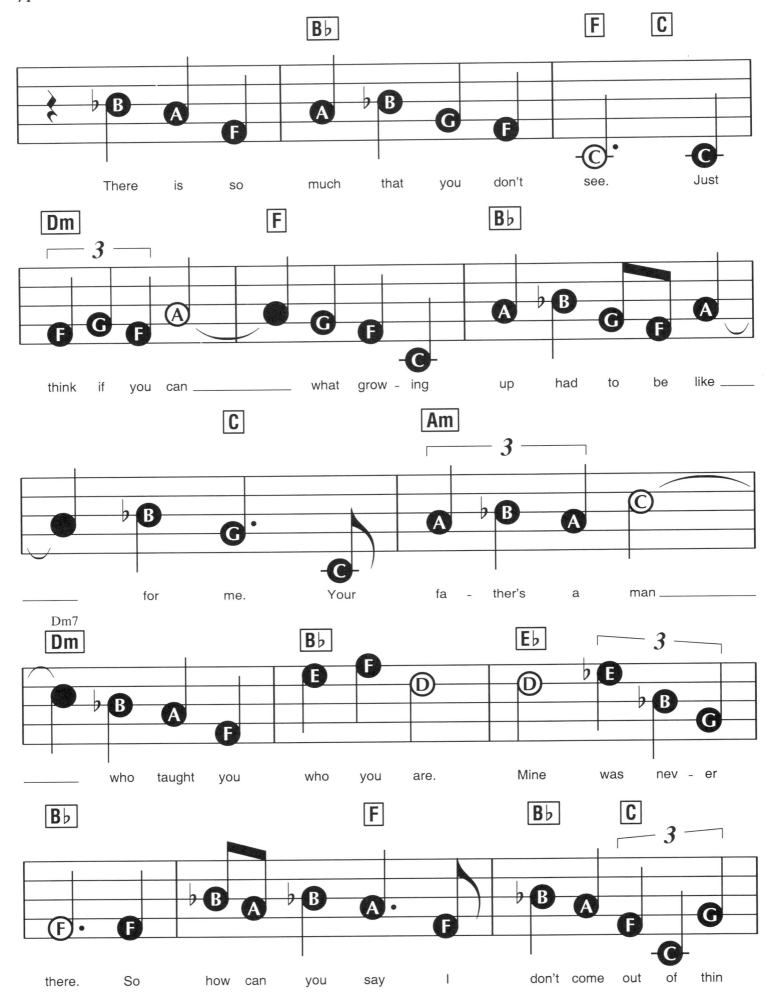

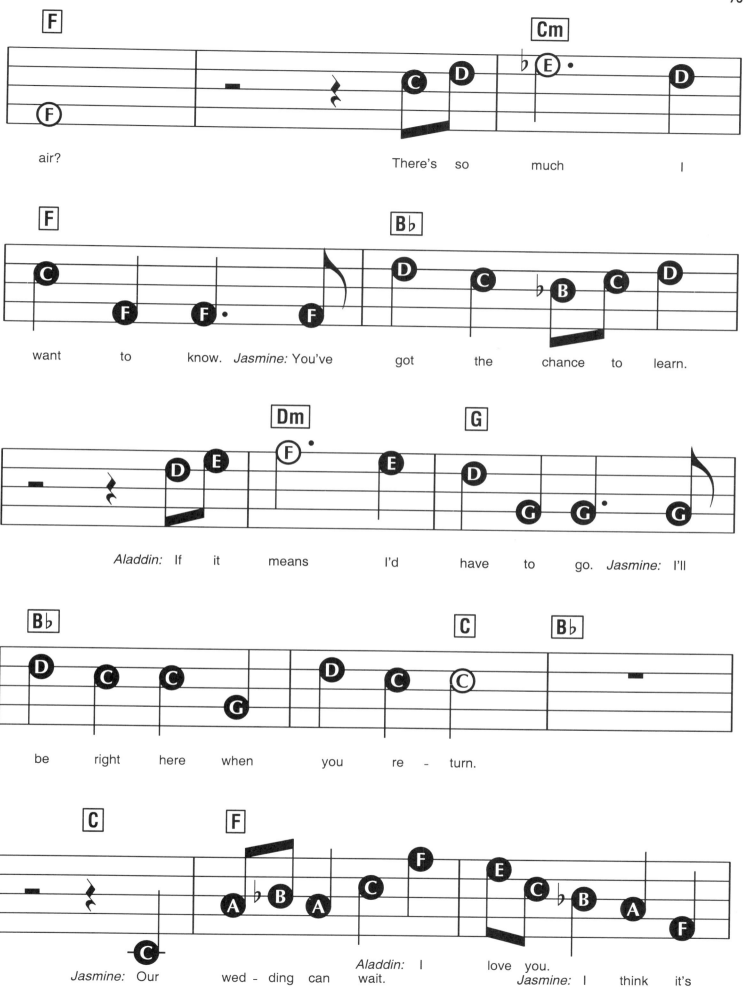

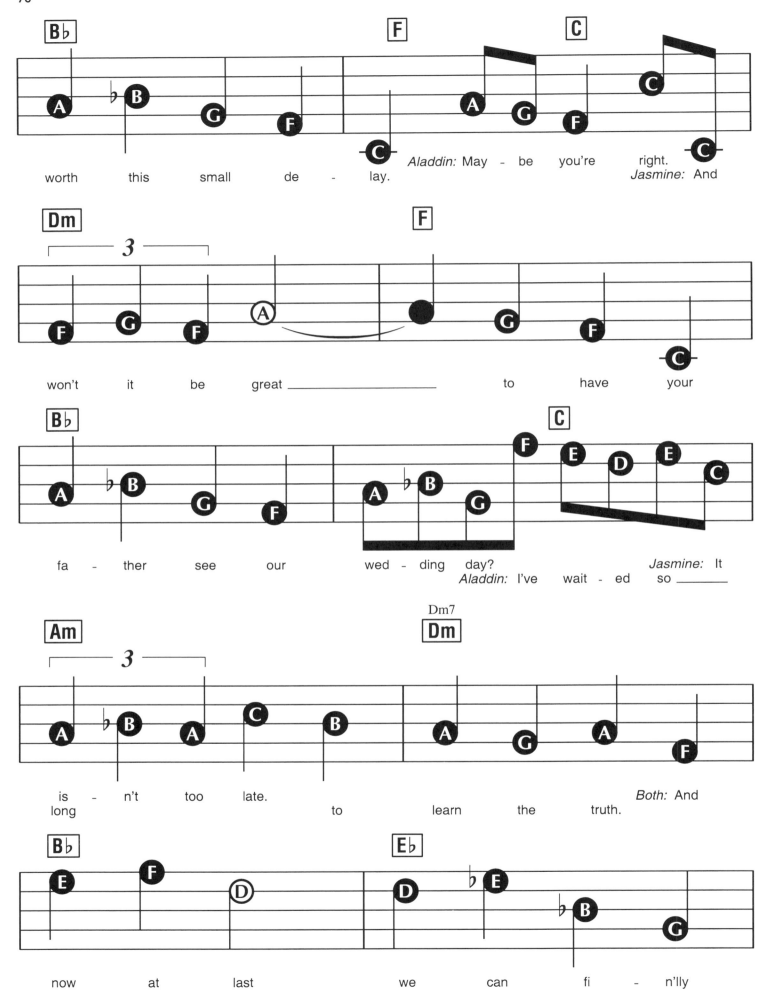

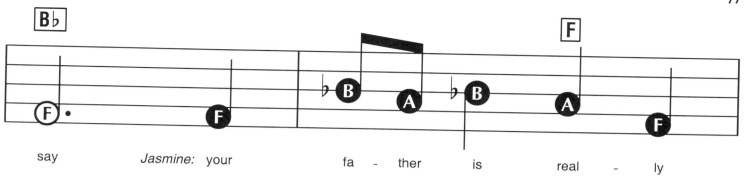

say   *Jasmine:* your   fa – ther   is   real – ly

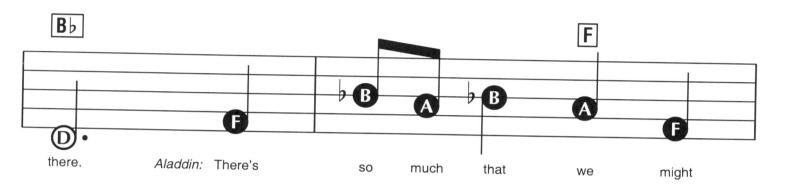

there.   *Aladdin:* There's   so   much   that   we   might

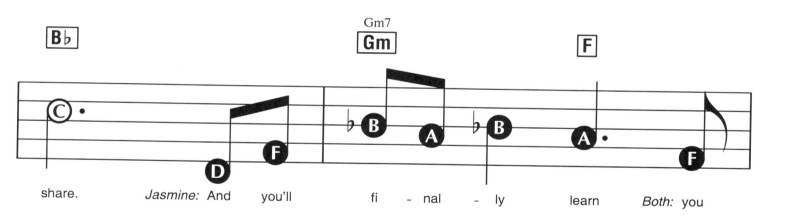

share.   *Jasmine:* And   you'll   fi – nal – ly   learn   *Both:* you

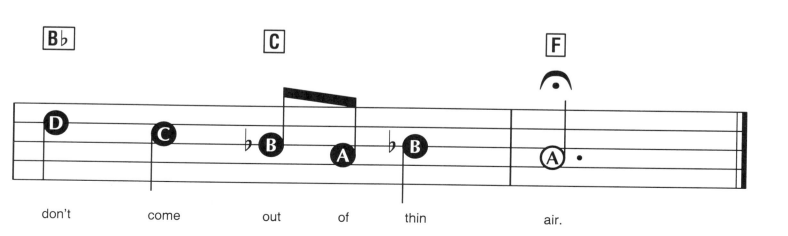

don't   come   out   of   thin   air.

OUT OF THIN AIR

(Aladdin and the King of Thieves)
Words and Music by David Friedman

Jasmine
You showed me the world
When I was all locked up inside.
You reached out your hand
And took me on a magic carpet ride.

One look at your smile
And I could see the light
Shining everywhere.
People like you
Don't come out of thin air.

Aladdin
You don't understand.
There is so much that you don't see.
Just think if you can
What growing up had to be like for me.
Your father's a man
Who taught you who you are.
Mine was never there.
So how can you say
I don't come out of thin air?

There's so much I want to know.

Jasmine
You've got the chance to learn.

Aladdin
If it means I'd have to go...

Jasmine
I'll be right here when you return.

Our wedding can wait.
(Aladdin: I love you.)
I think it's worth this small delay.
(Aladdin: Maybe you're right.)
And won't it be great
To have your father see our wedding day?
(Aladdin: I've waited so long)
It isn't too late.
(Aladdin: To learn the truth.)

Both
And now at last
We can finally say

Jasmine
Your father is really there.

Aladdin
There's so much that we might share.

Jasmine
And you'll finally learn

Both
You don't come out of thin air.

PART OF YOUR WORLD

(The Little Mermaid)
**Lyrics by Howard Ashman
Music by Alan Menken**

Look at this stuff. Isn't it neat?
Wouldn't you think my collection's complete?
Wouldn't you think I'm the girl,
The girl who has ev'rything.

Look at this trove, treasures untold.
How many wonders can one cavern hold?
Looking around here you'd think,
Sure, she's got ev'rything.

I've got gadgets and gizmos a-plenty.
I've got who-zits and what-zits galore.
You want thing-a-ma-bobs, I've got twenty.
But who cares? No big deal. I want more.

I wanna be where the people are.
I wanna see wanna see 'em dancin',
Walkin' around on those,
Whaddya call 'em, Oh, feet.

Flippin' your fins you don't get too far.
Legs are required for jumpin', dancin'.
Strollin' along down the,
What's that word again, Street.

Up where they walk, up where they run,
Up where they stay all day in the sun.
Wanderin' free, wish I could be
Part of that world.

What would I give if I could live
Outta these waters.
What would I pay to spend a day
Warm on the sand.

Betcha on land they understand.
Bet they don't reprimand their daughters.
Bright young women, sick of swimmin',
Ready to stand.

And ready to know what the people know.
Ask 'em my questions and get some answers.
What's a fire–and why does it,
What's the word, Burn.

When's it my turn?
Wouldn't I love, love to explore
That shore up above, out of the sea.
Wish I could be part of that world.

Part of Your World
from Walt Disney's THE LITTLE MERMAID

Registration 1
Rhythm: Pops or 8-Beat

Lyrics by Howard Ashman
Music by Alan Menken

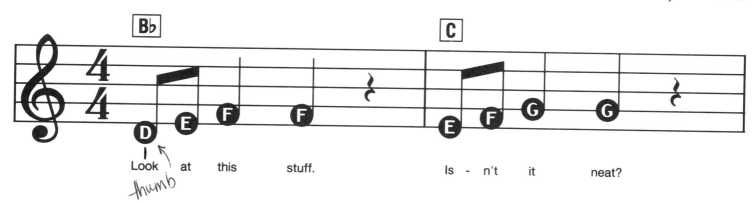

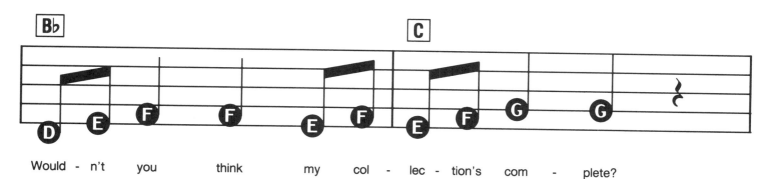

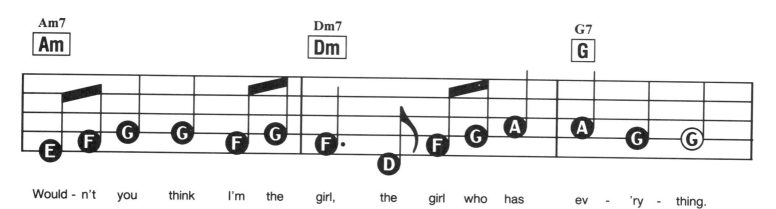

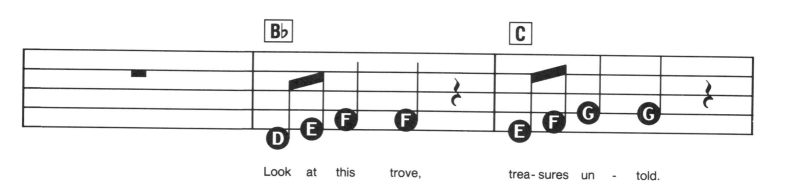

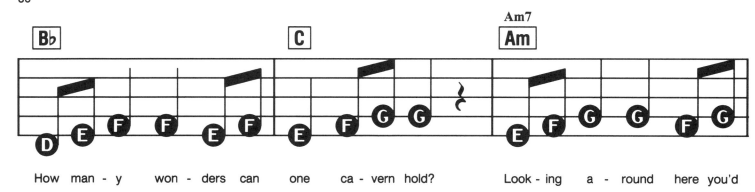

How man - y won - ders can one ca - vern hold? Look - ing a - round here you'd

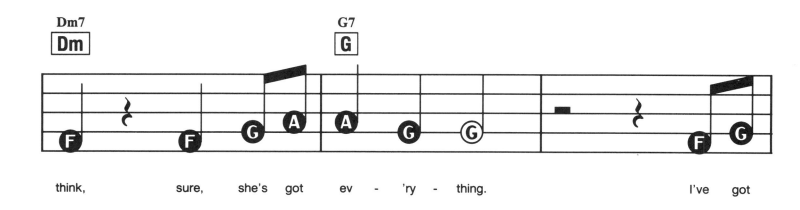

think, sure, she's got ev - 'ry - thing. I've got

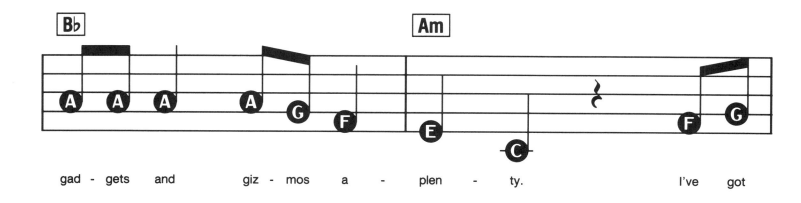

gad - gets and giz - mos a - plen - ty. I've got

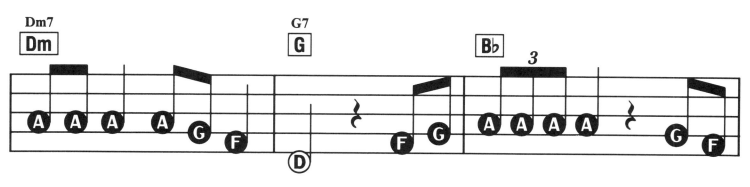

who - zits and what - zits ga - lore. You want thing - a - ma - bobs, I've got

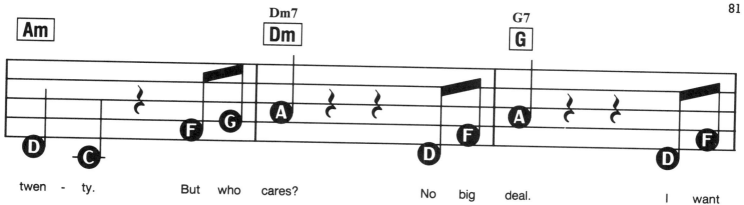

twen - ty. But who cares? No big deal. I want

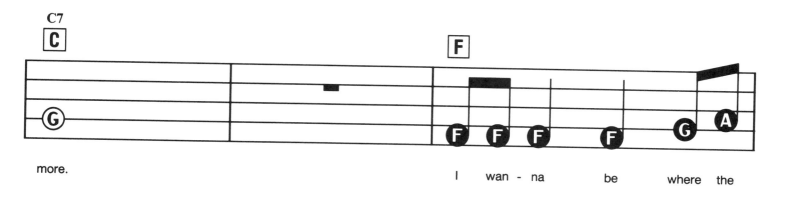

more. I wan - na be where the

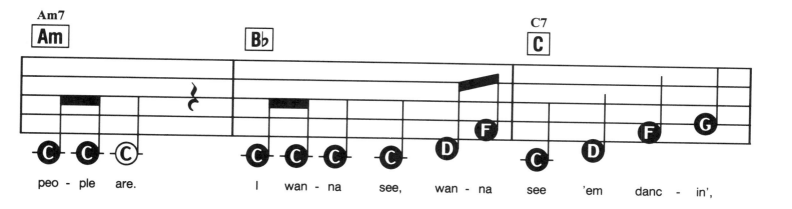

peo - ple are. I wan - na see, wan - na see 'em danc - in',

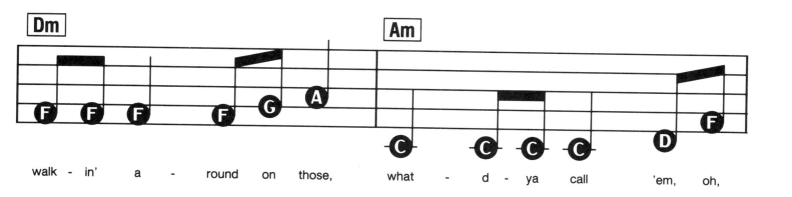

walk - in' a - round on those, what - d - ya call 'em, oh,

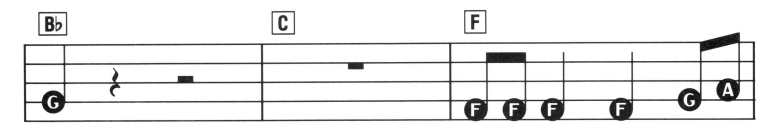

feet.   Flip - pin' your   fins   you don't

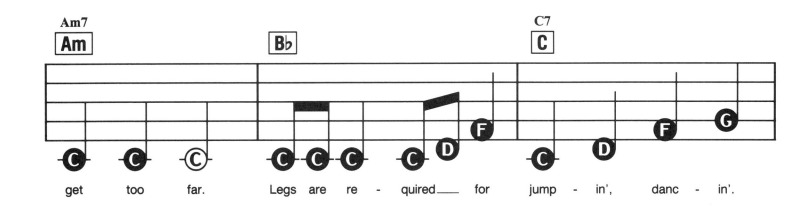

get   too   far.   Legs are   re - quired___ for   jump - in',   danc - in'.

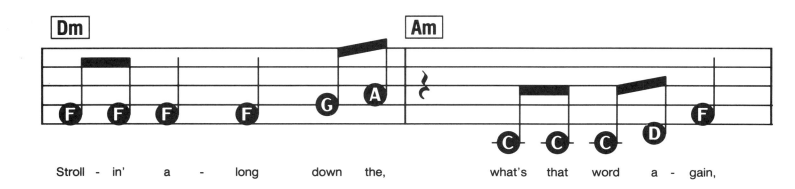

Stroll - in' a - long   down the,   what's that word a - gain,

street.   Up where they   walk,   up where they

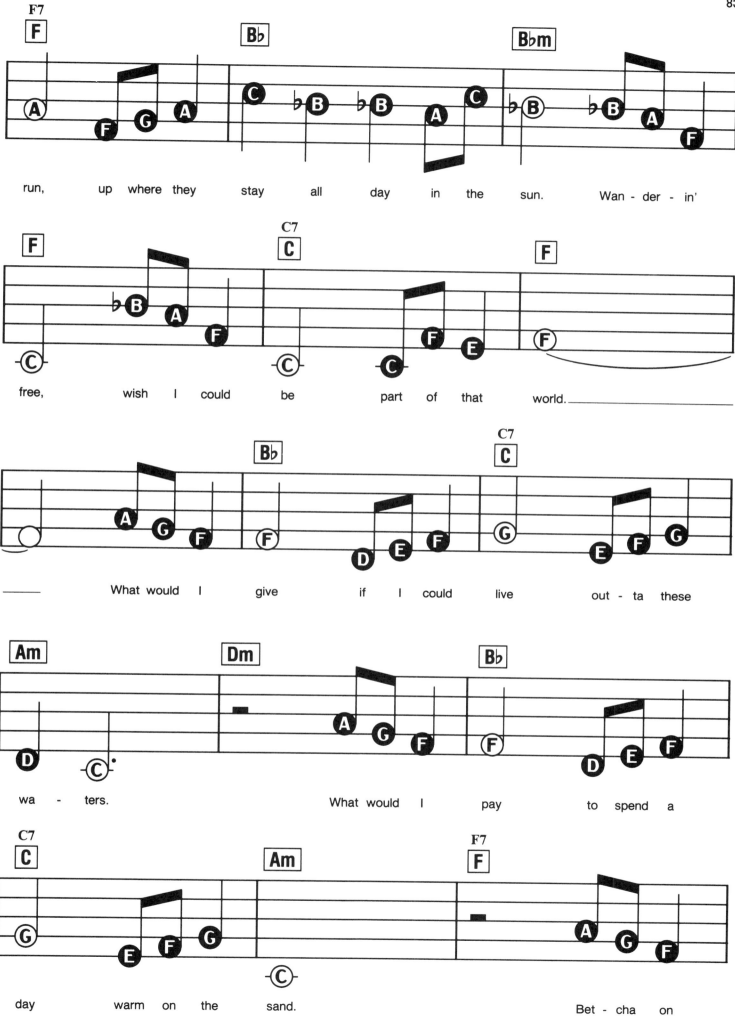

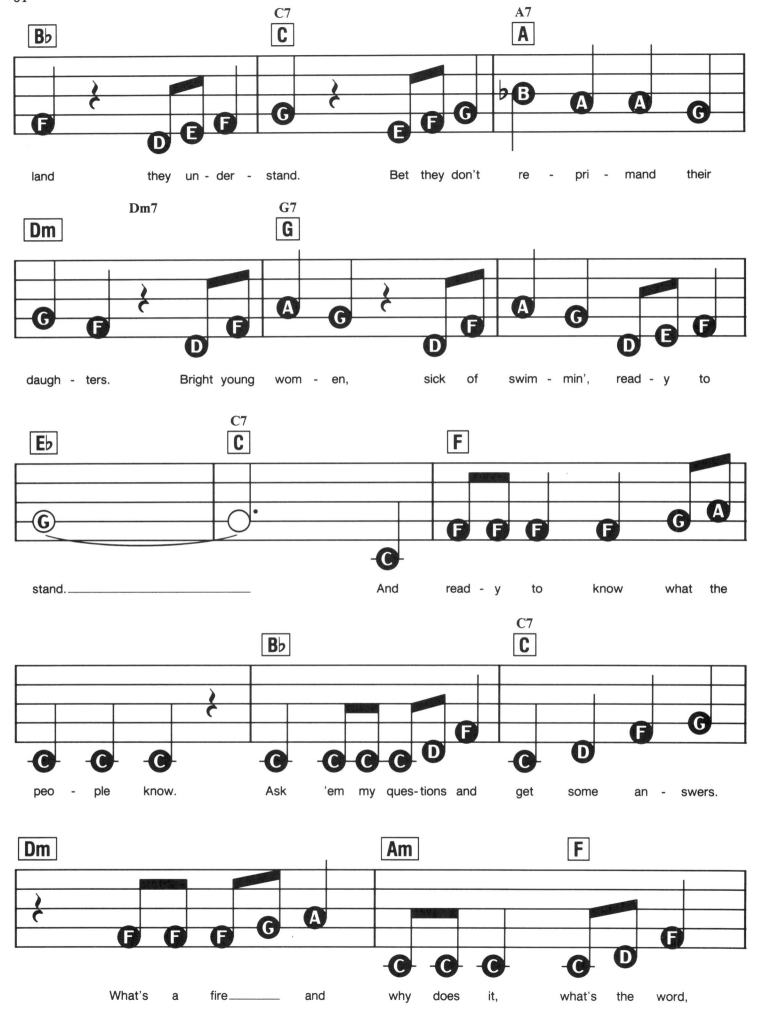

REFLECTION

(Mulan)
Music by Matthew Wilder
Lyrics by David Zippel

Look at me,
I will never pass for a perfect bride
Or a perfect daughter.
Can it be
I'm not meant to play this part?
Now I see
That if I were truly to be myself,
I would break my family's heart.

Who is that girl I see
Staring straight back at me?
Why is my reflection someone
I don't know?
Somehow I cannot hide
Who I am, though I've tried.
When will my reflection show
Who I am inside?
When will my reflection show
Who I am inside?

SLEEPING BEAUTY

(Sleeping Beauty)
Words by Tom Adair
Music by George Bruns

Sleeping Beauty fair,
Gold of sunshine in your hair,
Lips that shame the red, red rose,
Dreaming of true love in slumber repose.

One day he will come
Riding out of the dawn,
And you'll awaken to love's first kiss.
Till then, Sleeping Beauty, sleep on.

SO THIS IS LOVE

(Cinderella)
Words and Music by Mack David,
Al Hoffman and Jerry Livingston

So this is love, Mm
So this is love
So this is what makes life divine.
I'm all aglow, Mm
And now I know (And now I know)
The key to all heaven is mine.

My heart has wings, Mm
And I can fly,
I'll touch ev'ry star in the sky,
So this is the miracle that I've been dreaming of,
Mm, Mm, so this is love.

Reflection
from Walt Disney Pictures' MULAN

Registration 10
Rhythm: Ballad or 8 Beat

Music by Matthew Wilder
Lyrics by David Zippel

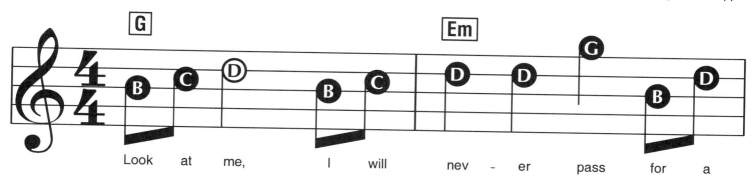

Look at me, I will nev – er pass for a

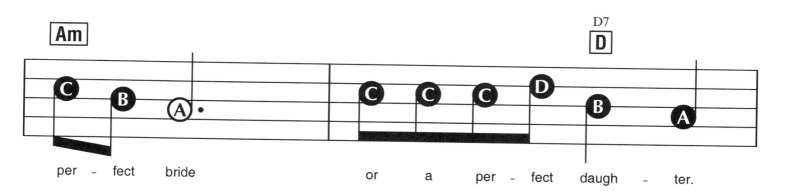

per – fect bride or a per – fect daugh – ter.

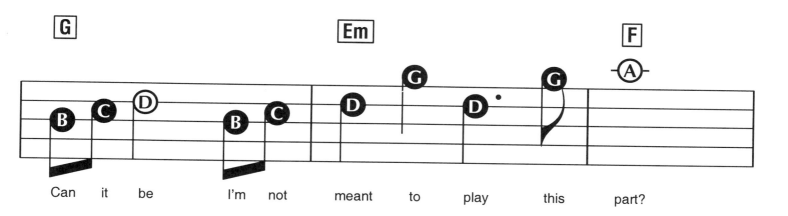

Can it be I'm not meant to play this part?

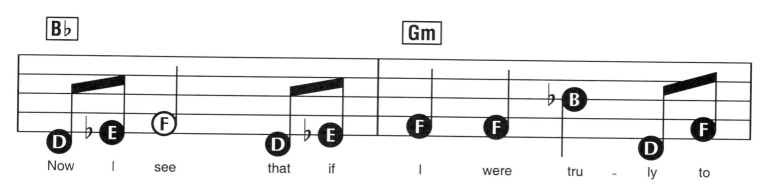

Now I see that if I were tru – ly to

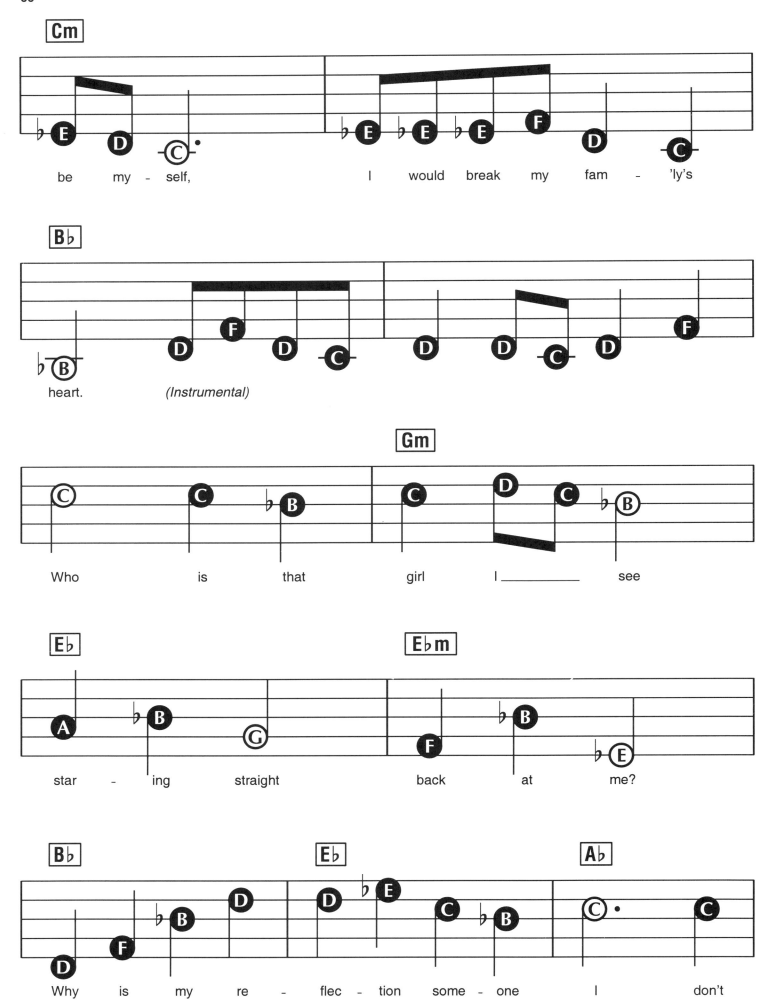

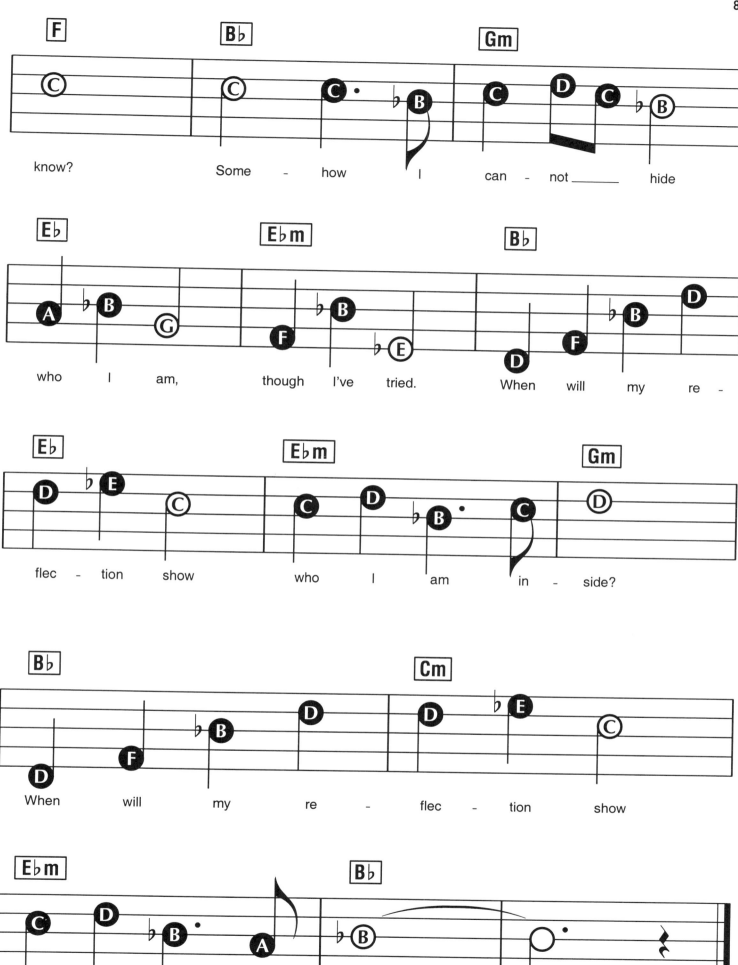

Sleeping Beauty
from Walt Disney's SLEEPING BEAUTY

Registration 4
Rhythm: Waltz

Words by Tom Adair
Music by George Bruns

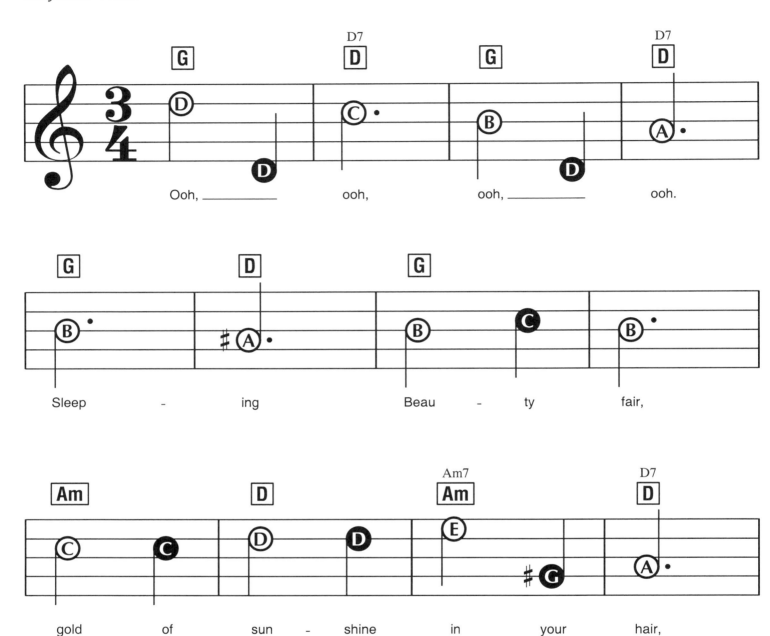

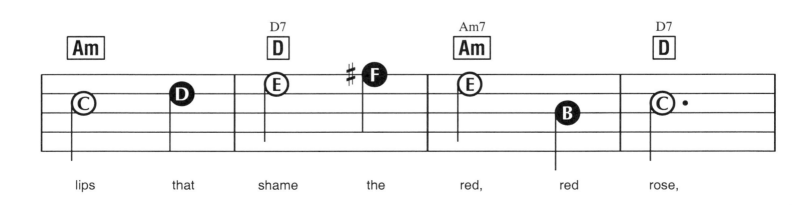

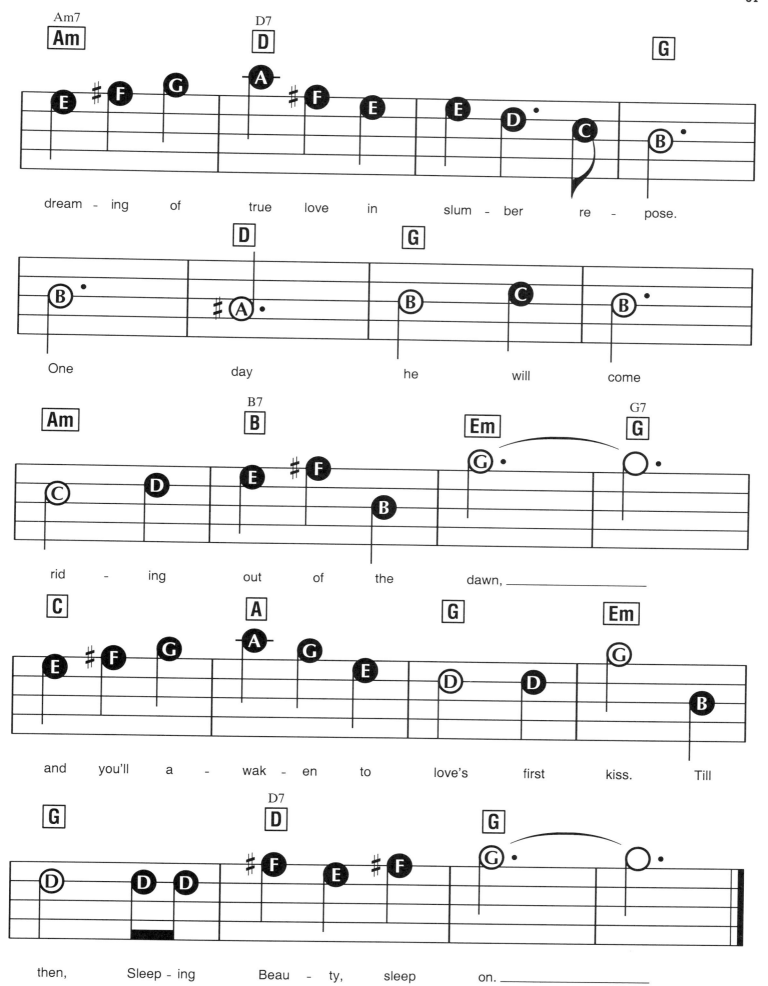

So This Is Love
(The Cinderella Waltz)
from Walt Disney's CINDERELLA

Registration 1
Rhythm: Waltz

Words and Music by Mack David,
Al Hoffman and Jerry Livingston

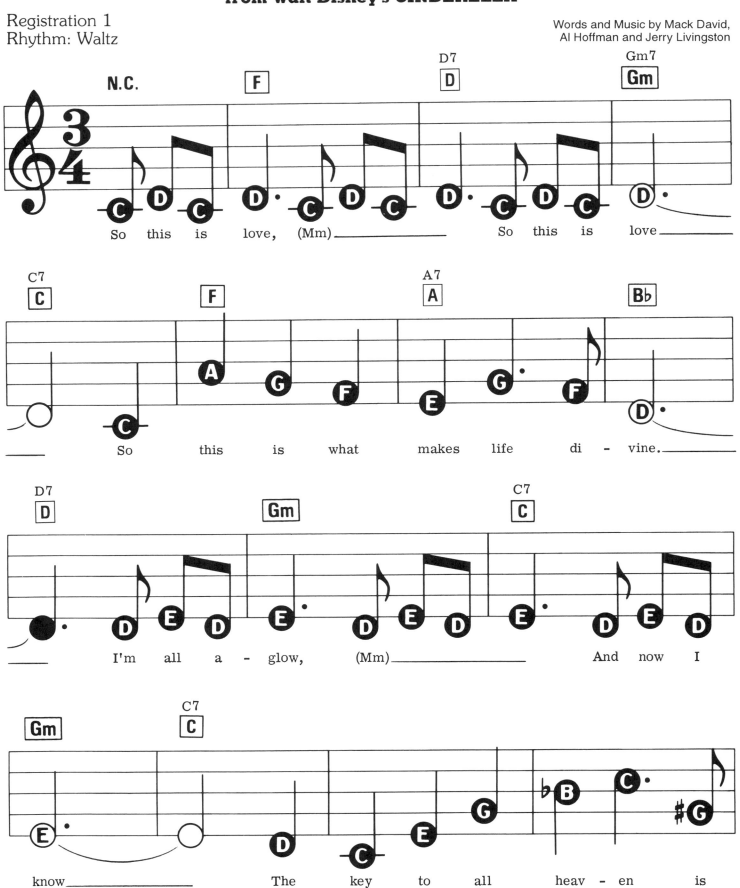

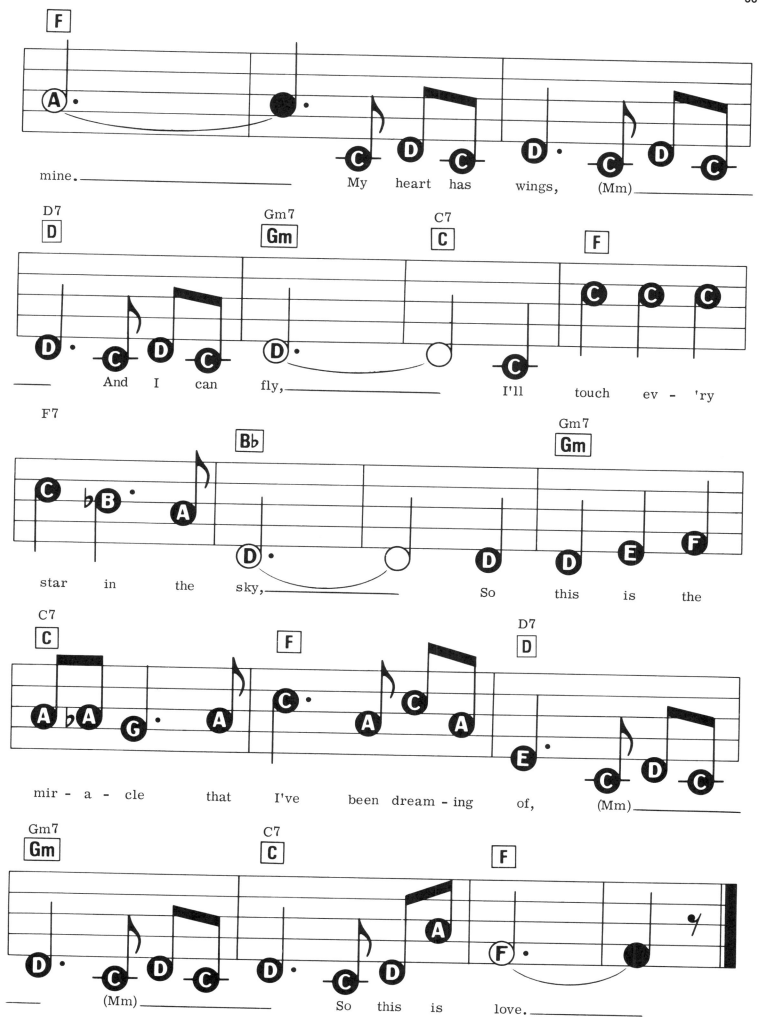

Something There

from Walt Disney's BEAUTY AND THE BEAST

Registration 7
Rhythm: 8 Beat or Pops

Lyrics by Howard Ashman
Music by Alan Menken

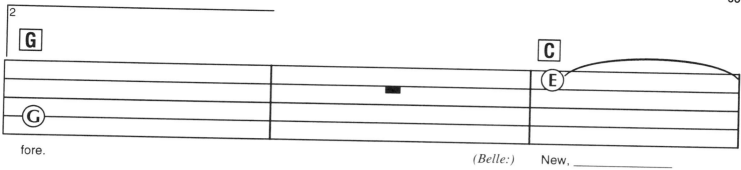

fore.

(Belle:)   New, _____

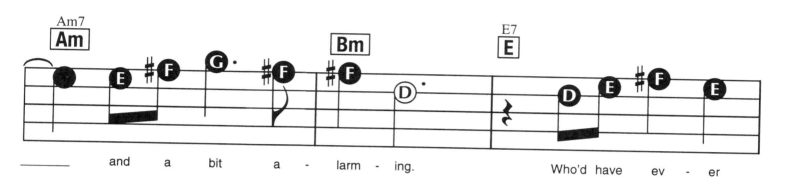

_____   and   a   bit   a - larm - ing.   Who'd   have   ev - er

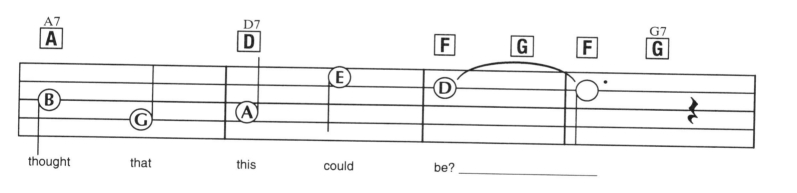

thought   that   this   could   be? _____

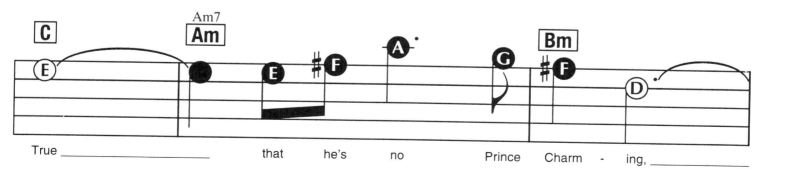

True _____   that   he's   no   Prince   Charm - ing, _____

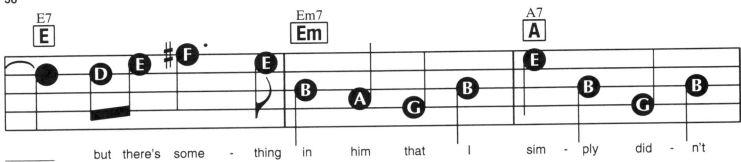

but there's some - thing in him that I sim - ply did - n't

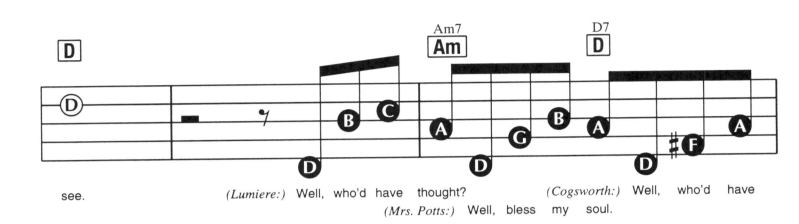

see.   (*Lumiere:*) Well, who'd have thought?   (*Cogsworth:*) Well, who'd have
                              (*Mrs. Potts:*) Well, bless my soul.

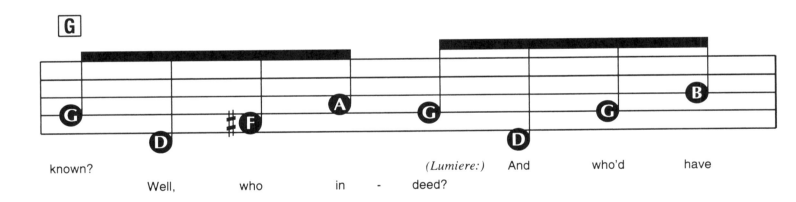

known?   Well, who in - deed?   (*Lumiere:*) And who'd have

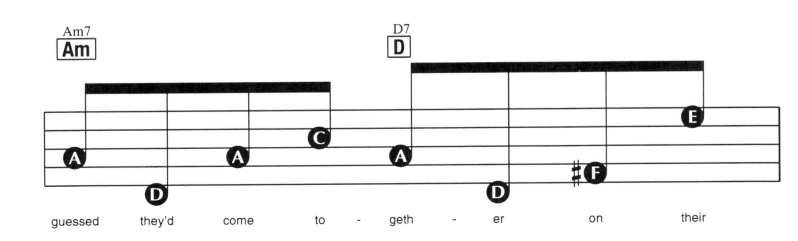

guessed they'd come to - geth - er on their

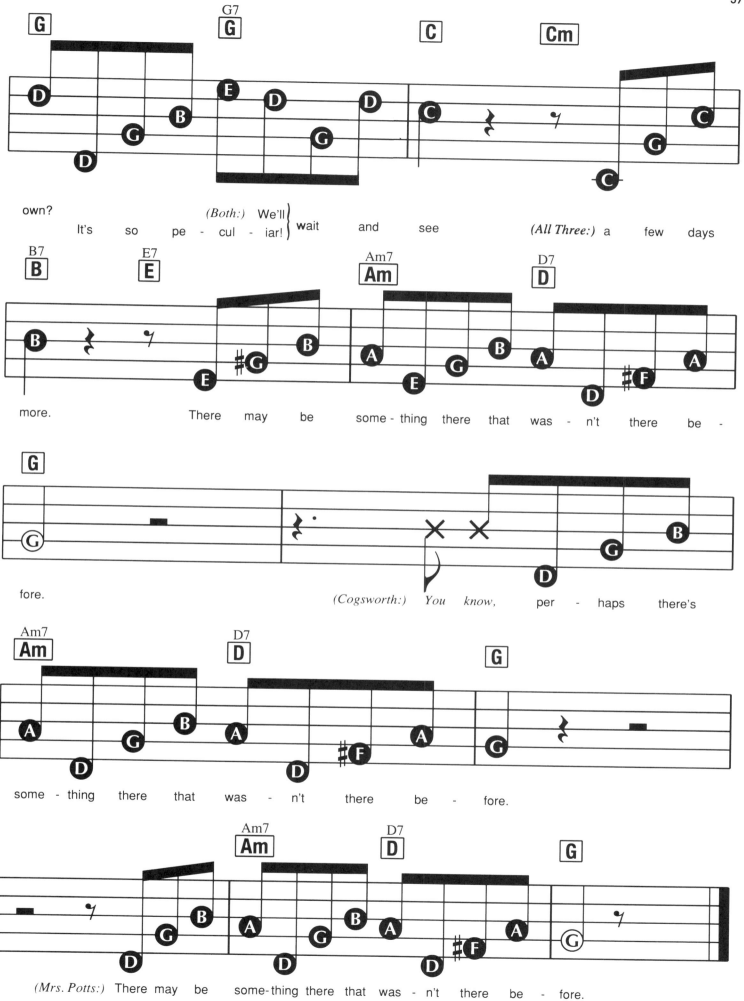

own? It's so pe - cul - iar! *(Both:)* We'll wait and see *(All Three:)* a few days more.

There may be some - thing there that was - n't there be - fore.

(Cogsworth:) You know, per - haps there's some - thing there that was - n't there be - fore.

(Mrs. Potts:) There may be some - thing there that was - n't there be - fore.

SOMETHING THERE

(Beauty and the Beast)
Lyrics by Howard Ashman
Music by Alan Menken

Belle
There's something sweet
And almost kind,
But he was mean and he was coarse and unrefined.
And now he's dear, and so unsure
I wonder why I didn't see it there before?

Beast
She glanced this way, I thought I saw.
And when we touched she didn't shudder at my paw.
No it can't be...I'll just ignore.
But then she's never looked at me that way before.

Belle
New, and a bit alarming.
Who'd have ever thought that this could be?
True that he's no Prince Charming,
But there's something in him
That I simply didn't see.

Lumiere
Well, who'd have thought?

Mrs. Potts
Well, bless my soul.

Cogsworth
Well, who'd have known?

Mrs. Potts
Well, who indeed?

Lumiere
And who'd have guessed they'd come
Together on their own?

Mrs. Potts
It's so peculiar.

Mrs. Potts/Lumiere/Cogsworth
We'll wait and see, a few days more.
There may be something there that
Wasn't there before.

Cogsworth
You know, perhaps there's is something there that
Wasn't there before.

Mrs. Potts
There may be something there that
Wasn't there before.

A WHOLE NEW WORLD
(Aladdin)
Music by Alan Menken
Lyrics by Tim Rice

Aladdin
I can show you the world,
Shining, shimmering, splendid.
Tell me, princess, now when did
You last let your heart decide?

I can open your eyes
Take you wonder by wonder
Over, sideways, and under
On a magic carpet ride.

A whole new world
A new fantastic point of view.
No one to tell us no
Or where to go
Or say we're only dreaming.

Jasmine
A whole new world
A dazzling place I never knew.
But when I'm way up here
It's crystal clear
That now I'm in a whole new world
With you.

Aladdin
Now I'm in a whole new world with you

Jasmine
Unbelievable sights
Indescribable feeling.
Soaring, tumbling, freewheeling
Through an endless diamond sky.
A whole new world
(Aladdin: Don't you dare close your eyes)
A hundred thousand things to see.
(Aladdin: Hold your breath—it gets better)

Jasmine
I'm like a shooting star.
I've come so far
I can't go back to where I used to be.

Aladdin
A whole new world
(Jasmine: Every turn a surprise)
With new horizons to pursue
(Jasmine: Every moment, red letter.)

Both
I'll chase them anywhere.
There's time to spare.
Let me share this whole new world with you.

Aladdin
A whole new world,
(Jasmine: A whole new world,)
That's where we'll be.
(Jasmine: That's where we'll be.)

Aladdin
A thrilling chase

Jasmine
A wondrous place

Both
For you and me.

A Whole New World
from Walt Disney's ALADDIN

Registration 1
Rhythm: 8-beat or Pops

Music by Alan Menken
Lyrics by Tim Rice

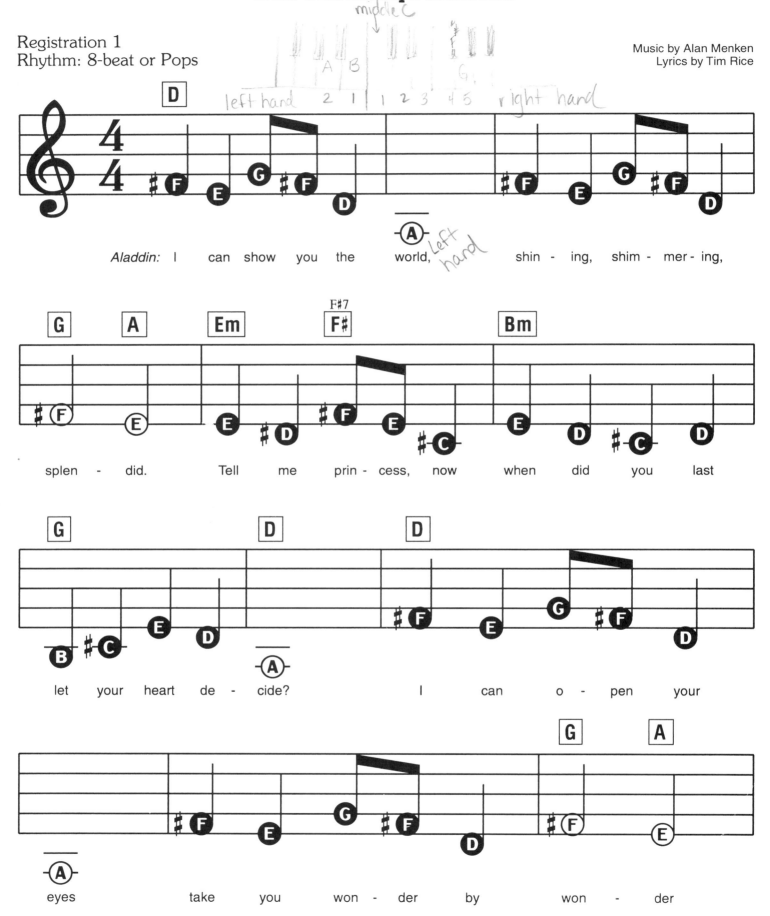

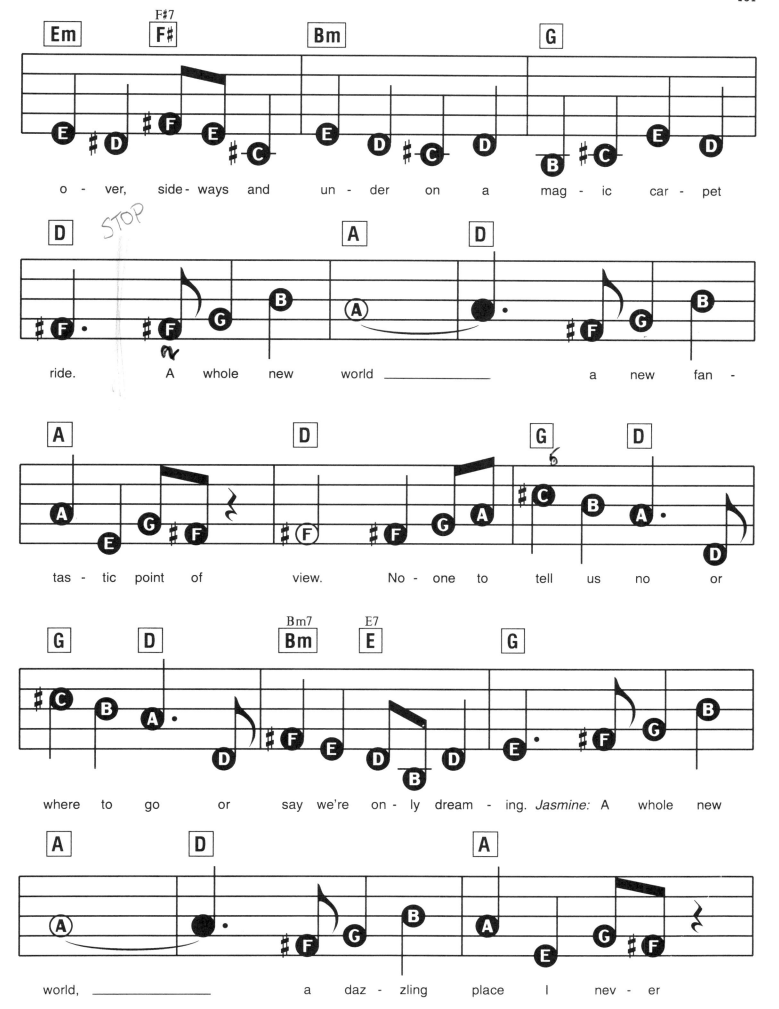

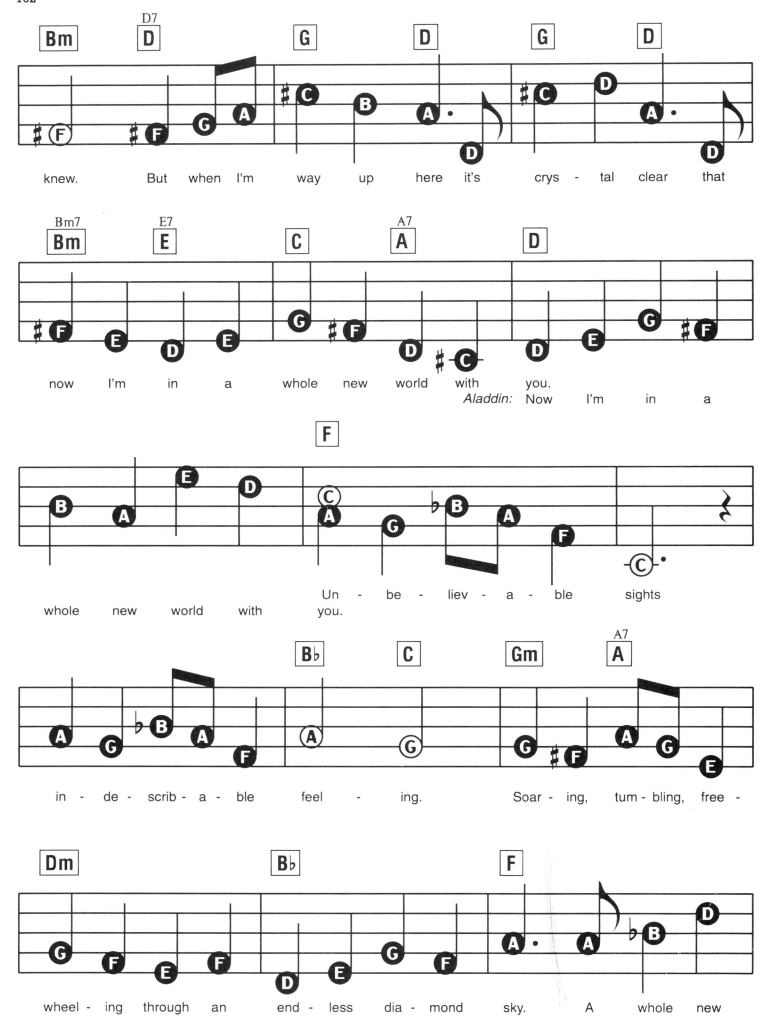

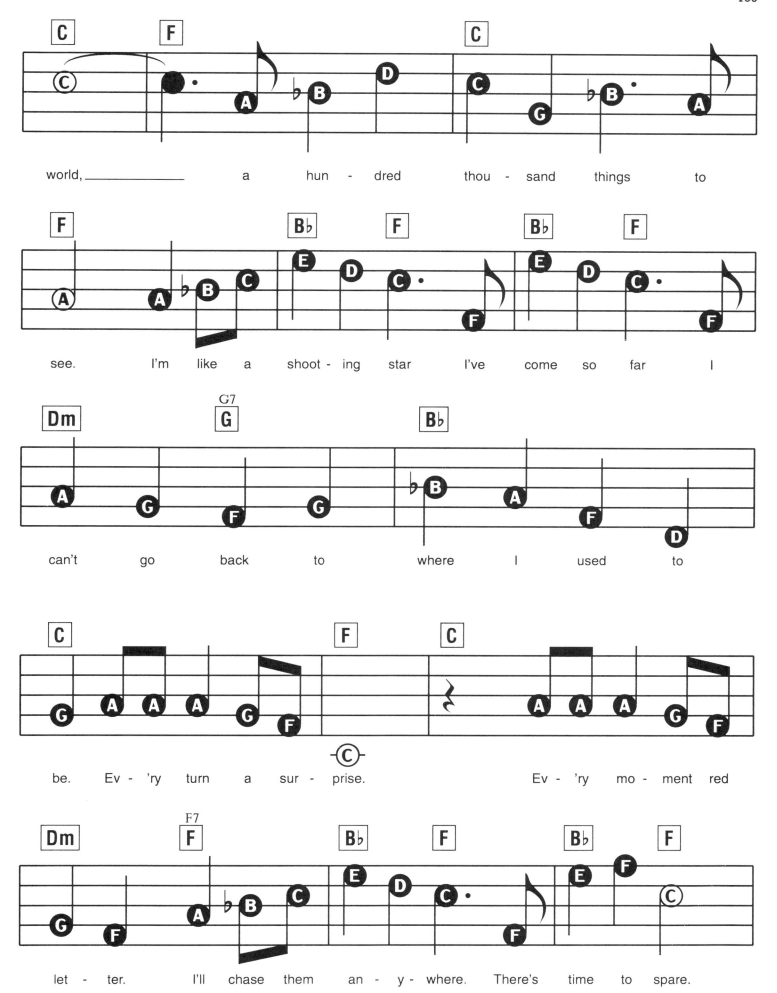

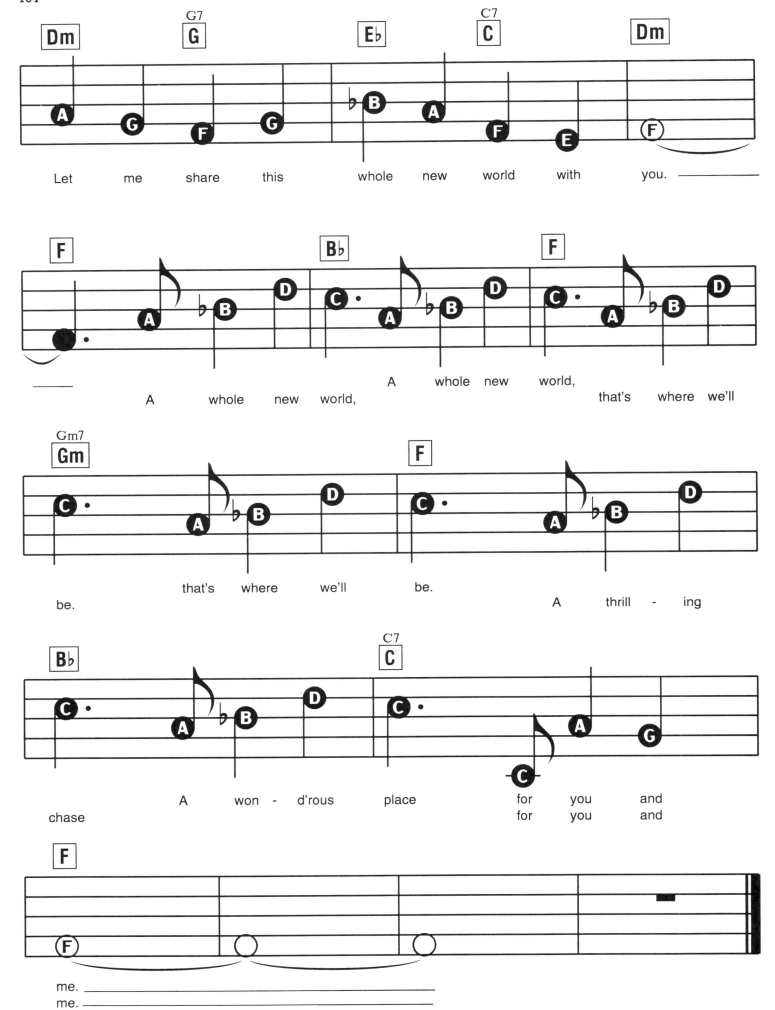